The Collegeville Psalter

for Sunday, Solemnities, and Major Feast Days

Paul Inwood

LITURGICAL PRESS
Collegeville, Minnesota

www.litpress.org

Reprint Policy

For your assistance, image files of the assembly responses are available online for you to download and reproduce in aids for worship. In order to reproduce these image files legally, you must either (1) purchase the Liturgical Press annual music reprint license (reporting the use of titles is not required) or (2) have a membership with the licensing agent Onelicense.net (reporting the use of titles is mandatory).

The image files can be found at the following web address: www.litpress.org/tcp_responses.

ACKNOWLEDGMENTS

Cover design: Monica Bokinskie. Photo by Michael Becker.

ISBN: 978-0-8146-4616-8

The Collegeville Psalter

In presenting a new psalter for parish use for the Sundays and major feast days of the three-year Lectionary cycle, I have had two basic aims in mind:

(a) to provide responses for the assembly that are accessible and memorable;
(b) to provide psalm tones for cantors that are interesting and rewarding;
while all the time maintaining the essential simplicity of the *Basilica Psalter*.

This book follows the current U.S. Lectionary text faithfully. The psalm verses are as printed there, using the New American Bible translation of scripture. The responses are also as printed there, using the ICEL (International Commission on English in the Liturgy) text currently in use, with occasional repetition of verbal phrases for the purposes of memorability and ease of singing. Errors occurring in the U.S. Lectionary text are noted but not corrected (except for obvious typos).

At the time of writing it seems that it may be as long as ten years before a new edition of the U.S. Lectionary is available. When a new edition is published, it will be easy to adapt the psalm tones included in this book to the text of the Revised Grail Psalter (RGP), if and when that text is eventually finalized. The responses should also prove easy to adapt to new responses derived from the RGP.

In addition to all the Sundays and feast days that can replace the Sunday celebration, I have included the psalms from the "Common Texts" section of the Lectionary. These psalms may be used to substitute for the psalm of the day on a seasonal basis, as provided for in the Lectionary (cf. *General Introduction to the Lectionary for Mass*, para 89).

The psalm tones, with very few exceptions, use a simple reciting note + termination format. Attention is drawn to the pointing. The first word or syllable to leave the reciting note is indicated by underlining.

In general, the last note of the termination will coincide with the last strong syllable of the line. Most people are used to there being one subsidiary syllable following the main syllable on the final note of the termination. In this psalter you will find a number of instances of two or even three subsidiary syllables following the main syllable on the final note of the termination.

For example, in Psalm 8, verse 1, the final line is pointed
    or the son of man that <u>you</u> should care for him?
and not
    or the son of man that you should <u>care</u> for him?
showing that the last strong syllable of the line should be "care" and not "him."

Similarly, in Psalm 34, verse 2, line 3, you will find
    I sought the LORD, <u>and</u> he answered me
and not
    I sought the LORD, and he <u>an</u>swered me
showing that the last strong syllable of the line should be the "an" of "answered" and not "me."

Please follow the pointing as given, even if it seems unfamiliar or uneasy. If given the opportunity, most should get used to this more nuanced style rather quickly. If more than one word or syllable is underlined, they are sung to the same note of the termination.

The line layout of the NAB psalm verses has sometimes been modified for the purposes of fitting text with psalm tone:

A lightly indented line indicates text that occupies a new line in the original. This line and the preceding line are sung to the same measure of the tone. (Exception: Ps 136, where the indented line has its own melodic mini-refrain.)

A heavily indented line indicates text that is part of the preceding line in the original. If there are two underlined words or syllables, one in each line, the two lines are sung to successive measures of the tone. If there is only one underlining, the runover has been caused by a line that is too long to fit, and both lines are sung to the same measure of the tone.

Asterisks are used to show omitted measures of the tone: one asterisk indicates one omitted measure, two asterisks indicates two omitted measures. The single instance of a § symbol (Ps 139) indicates an inserted measure.

Where a psalm has a number of different responses, similar musical material is used for all of them. The psalm tone for each psalm is designed to go with the response(s), either by using similar tonality (the majority of cases), or occasionally with a deliberate contrast called for by the nature of the psalm itself. Some psalm tones consist of two elements repeated to make a four-line chant (though with a varied harmonization on the repetition). A small number of psalm tones contain palindromes — the same notes either forwards or backwards. Some psalm tones are used several times throughout the book, occasionally in different keys or modalities, and even with some modifications where required by the psalm text.

If two notes in the left hand are difficult or impossible to play as written, the upper note can always be taken by the right hand. Sometimes a right-hand note is easier when taken by the left hand. Throughout the book it will often be found helpful or necessary to divide the inner accompaniment parts between the hands.

To economize on paper, different extracts of the same psalm text will frequently be found printed on the same page. The headings will show which verses to select on any given day, but, to avoid confusion, in complex cases users will also find boxes that set out the verses allocated to each day in an easy-to-follow format.

At the back of the book are indexes of psalm tones and an index of liturgical use. To find the psalm assigned for any given occasion, go to the index of liturgical use. To locate psalm tones by key or melodic shape, use the numerical index of psalm tones or the index of psalm tones by category. This will also enable the tones to be used with other psalms not included in this book.

The psalms are printed in the book in numerical order, followed by the canticles in biblical sequence, so there is no need for a numerical index of psalms. There are, however, indexes of first lines of responses and first lines of psalms.

Paul Inwood
December 2017

Psalm 1

6th Sunday in Ordinary Time, Year C

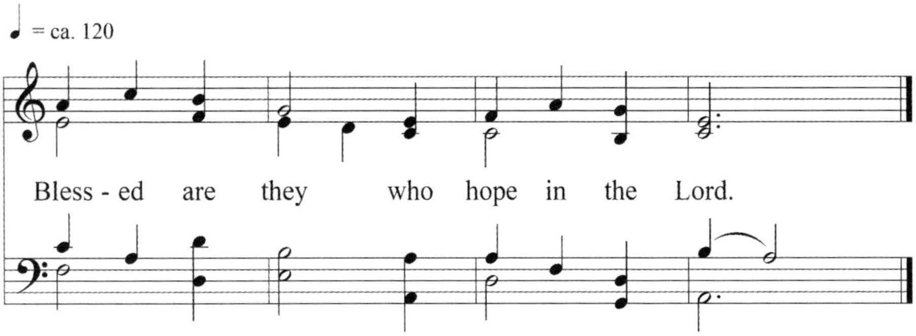

Psalm Tone

Psalm 1:1-2, 3, 4 and 6. R/ 40:5a

1. Blessed the man who follows not
   the counsel of the wicked,
   nor walks in the way of sinners,
   nor sits in the company of the insolent,
   but delights in the law of the LORD
   and meditates on his law day and night. *R/*

2. He is like a tree
   planted near running water,
   that yields its fruit in due season,
   and whose leaves never fade.
   [*Omit m. 5*]
   * Whatever he does, prospers. *R/*

3. Not so the wicked, not so;
   they are like chaff which the wind drives away.
   For the LORD watches over the way of the just,
   but the way of the wicked vanishes. *R/*
   ** [*Omit mm. 5-6*]

Psalm 4

3rd Sunday of Easter, Year B

3rd Sunday of Easter, Year B, *alternate response*

Psalm Tone *Psalm 4:2, 4, 7-8, 9. R/. v. 7a*

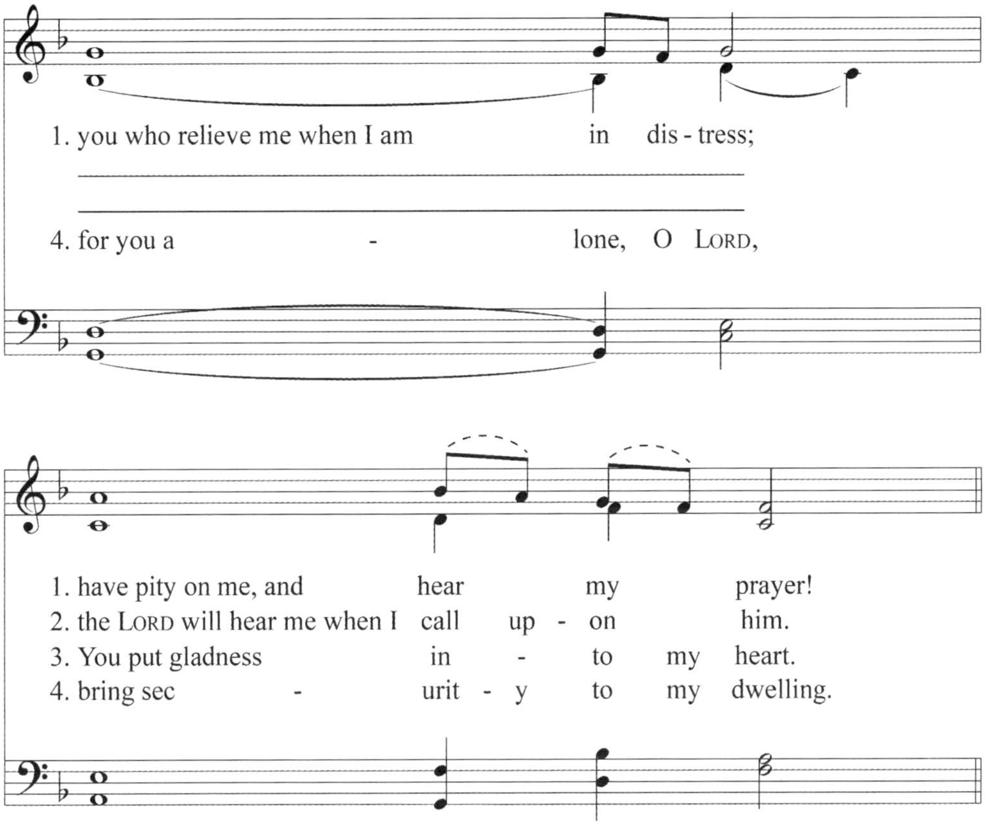
1. you who relieve me when I am in dis - tress;
4. for you a - lone, O LORD,
1. have pity on me, and hear my prayer!
2. the LORD will hear me when I call up - on him.
3. You put gladness in - to my heart.
4. bring sec - urit - y to my dwelling.

Psalm 8

Trinity Sunday, Year C

Psalm Tone

Psalm 8:4-5, 6-7, 8-9. R/ v. 2a

1. When I behold your heavens, the work of your fingers,
   the moon and the stars which you set in place —
   what is man that you should be mindful of him,
   or the son of man that you should care for him? *R/*

2. You have made him little less than the angels,
   and crowned him with glory and honor.
   You have given him rule over the works of your hands,
   putting all things under his feet. *R/*

3. All sheep and oxen,
   yes, and the beasts of the field,
   the birds of the air, the fishes of the sea,
   and whatever swims the paths of the seas. *R/*

Psalm 15

22nd Sunday in Ordinary Time, Year B

* *Some editions of the Lectionary begin this response* "One who does justice..."

16th Sunday in Ordinary Time, Year C

Psalm Tone

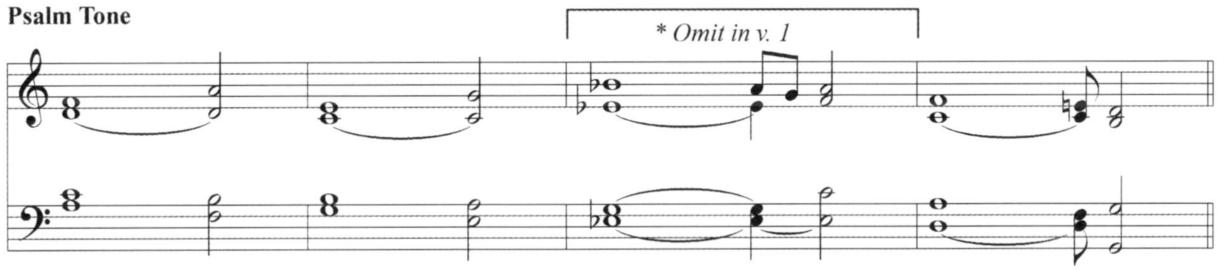

Psalm 15:2-3, 3-4, 4-5. R/ v. 1a

22 OT B only

1. Whoever walks blamelessly and does justice;
   who thinks the truth in his heart
   * and slanders not with his tongue. *R/*

2. Who harms not his fellow man,
   nor takes up a reproach against his neighbor;
   by whom the reprobate is despised,
   while he honors those who fear the LORD. *R/*

3. Who lends not his money at usury
   and accepts no bribe against the innocent.
   Whoever does these things
   shall never be disturbed. *R/*

16 OT C only

1a. Who walks blamelessly and does justice;
   who thinks the truth in his heart
   * and slanders not with his tongue. *R/*

Psalm 16

Easter Vigil 2 • 33rd Sunday in Ordinary Time, Year B • 13th Sunday in Ordinary Time, Year C

** 33 OT B has an exclamation point at the end of the Response instead of a period.*

3rd Sunday of Easter, Year A

3rd Sunday of Easter, Year A, *alternate response*

Psalm Tone

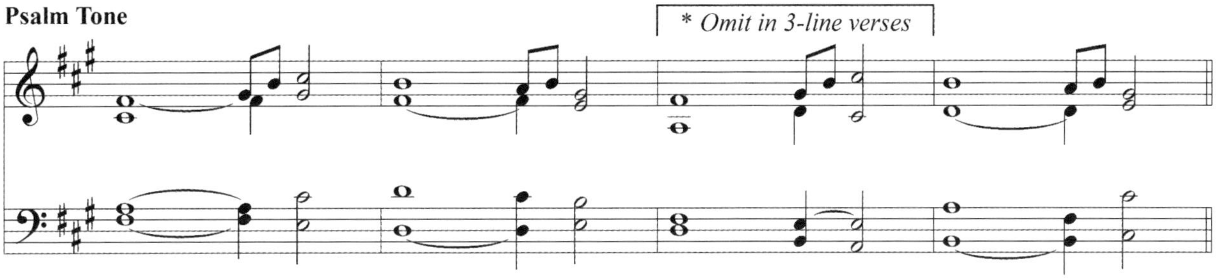

Psalm 16:5, 8, 9-10, 11. R/ v. 1

Easter Vigil 2 and 33 OT B only

1. O LORD, my allotted portion and my cup,
   you it is who hold fast my lot.
   I set the LORD ever before me;
   with him at my right hand I shall not be disturbed. *R/*

Psalm 16:1-2, 5, 7-8, 9-10, 11. R. v. 1; v. 11a

3 Easter A and 13 OT C only

1. Keep me, O God, for in you I take refuge;
   I say to the LORD, "My Lord are you.
   O LORD, my allotted portion and my cup,
   you it is who hold fast my lot." *R/*

1a. I bless the LORD who counsels me;
   even in the night my heart exhorts me.
   I set the LORD ever before me;
   with him at my right hand I shall not be disturbed. *R/*

2. Therefore my heart is glad and my soul rejoices,
   my body, too, abides in confidence;
   because you will not abandon my soul to the netherworld,
   nor will you suffer your faithful one to undergo corruption. *R/*

3. You will show me the path to life,
   fullness of joys in your presence,
   * [*Omit m. 3*]
   the delights at your right hand forever. *R/*

Psalm 17

32nd Sunday in Ordinary Time, Year C

Psalm Tone

Psalm 17:1, 5-6, 8, 15. R/ v. 15b

1. Hear, O Lord, a just suit;
   attend to my outcry;
   hearken to my prayer
   from lips without deceit. *R/*

2. My steps have been steadfast in your paths,
   my feet have not faltered.
   I call upon you, for you will answer me, O God;
   incline your ear to me; hear my word. *R/*

3. Keep me as the apple of your eye,
   hide me in the shadow of your wings.
   But I in justice shall behold your face;
   on waking I shall be content in your presence. *R/*

Psalm 18

30th Sunday in Ordinary Time, Year A • 31st Sunday in Ordinary Time, Year B

Psalm Tone

Psalm 18:2-3, 3-4, 47, 51. R/ v. 2

1. ** I love you, O Lord, my strength,
   O Lord, my rock, my fortress, my deliverer. *R/*

2. My God, my rock of refuge,
   my shield, the horn of my salvation, my stronghold!
   Praised be the Lord, I exclaim,
   and I am safe from my enemies. *R/*

3. The Lord lives and blessed be my rock!
   Extolled be God my savior.
   You who gave great victories to your king
   and showed kindness to your anointed. *R/*

(In the Lectionary, verse 3 has minor differences of punctuation on the two Sundays, but the wording is identical.)

Psalm 19

3rd Sunday of Lent, Year B • Easter Vigil 6 • Pentecost Vigil 2, *alternate psalm* • Common Ordinary Time 1

3rd Sunday in Ordinary Time, Year C • 15th Sunday in Ordinary Time Year C, *alternate psalm* • Common Ordinary Time 1, *alternate response*

26th Sunday in Ordinary Time, Year B

Psalm Tone

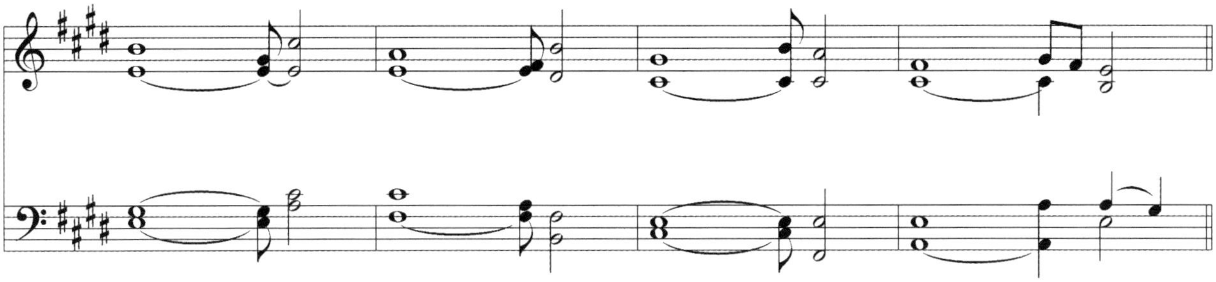

Psalm 19:8, 9, 10, 11. R/ John 6:68c; John 6:63c; Ps 19:9a.

1. The law of the LORD is perfect,
 refreshing the soul;
 the decree of the LORD is trustworthy,
 giving wisdom to the simple. *R/*

2. The precepts of the LORD are right,
 rejoicing the heart;
 the command of the LORD is clear,
 enlightening the eye. *R/*

3. The fear of the LORD is pure,
 enduring forever;
 the ordinances of the LORD are true,
 all of them just. *R/*

4. They are more precious than gold,
 than a heap of purest gold;
 sweeter also than syrup
 or honey from the comb. *R/*

(In the Lectionary, there are minor differences of punctuation in verses 1 and 2, but the wording is identical.)

26 OT B *Verses 1 and 3 opposite, then:*

3a. Though your servant is careful of them,
 very diligent in keeping them,
 yet who can detect failings?
 Cleanse me from my unknown faults! *R/*

4a. From wanton sin especially, restrain your servant;
 let it not rule over me.
 Then shall I be blameless and innocent
 of serious sin. *R/*

3 OT C *Verses 1-2 opposite, then:*

3b. Let the words of my mouth
 and the thought of my heart
 find favor before you,
 O LORD, my rock and my redeemer. *R/*

3 Lent B, Easter Vigil 6, Pentecost Vigil 2 alt., 15 OT C alt., Common OT 1
1. - 2. - 3. - 4.
26 OT B
1 - 3. - 3a. - 4a.
3 OT C
1. - 2. - 3b.

Saints Peter and Paul Vigil

Psalm Tone

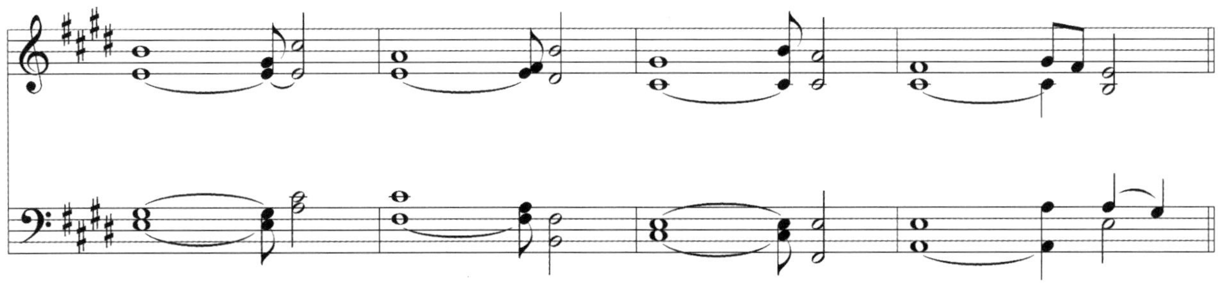

Psalm 19:2-3, 4-5. R/ v. 5

1. The heavens declare the glory of God,
   and the firmament proclaims his handiwork.
   Day pours out the word to day,
   and night to night imparts knowledge. *R/*

2. Not a word nor a discourse
   whose voice is not heard;
   through all the earth their voice resounds,
   and to the ends of the world, their message. *R/*

Psalm 22

Palm Sunday • Common Holy Week

Psalm Tone

Psalm 22:8-9, 17-18, 19-20, 23-24. R./ v. 2a

1. All who see me scoff at me;
they mock me with parted lips, they wag their heads:
"He relied on the Lord; let him deliver him,
let him rescue him, if he loves him." *R/*

2. Indeed, many dogs surround me,
a pack of evildoers closes in upon me;
they have pierced my hands and my feet;
I can count all my bones. *R/*

3. They divide my garments among them,
and for my vesture they cast lots.
But you, O Lord, be not far from me;
O my help, hasten to aid me. *R/*

4. I will proclaim your name to my brethren;
in the midst of the assembly I will praise you:
"You who fear the Lord, praise him;
[*Repeat m. 3*] all you descendants of Jacob, give glory to him;
revere him, all you descendants of Israel!" *R/*

5th Sunday of Easter, Year B

5th Sunday of Easter, *alternate response*

Psalm Tone

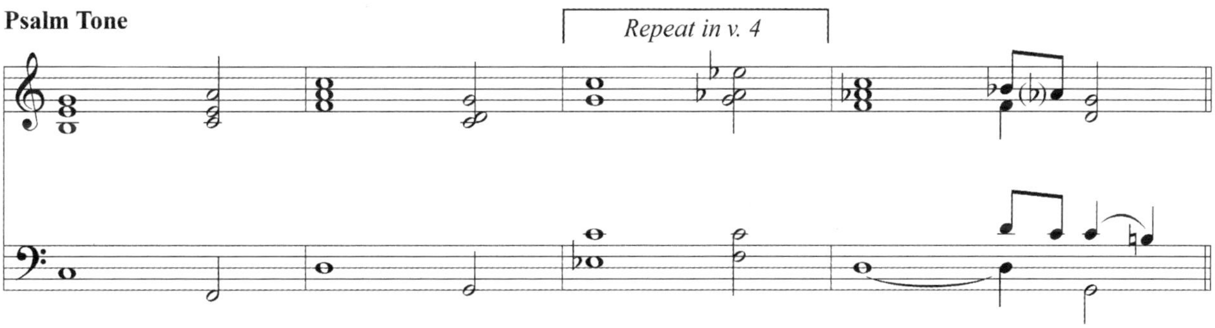

Psalm 22:26-27, 28, 30, 31-32. R/ v. 26a

1. I will fulfill my vows before those who fear the Lord.
   The lowly shall eat their fill;
   they who seek the Lord shall praise him:
   "May your hearts live forever!" *R/*

2. All the ends of the earth
   shall remember and turn to the Lord;
   all the families of the nations
   shall bow down before him. *R/*

3. To him alone shall bow down
   all who sleep in the earth;
   before him shall bend
   all who go down into the dust. *R/*

4. And to him my soul shall live;
   my descendants shall serve him.
   Let the coming generation be told of the Lord
   [*Repeat m. 3*] that they may proclaim to a people yet to be born
   the justice he has shown. *R/*

Psalm 23

4th Sunday of Lent, Year A • 4th Sunday of Easter, Year A • Christ the King, Year A • 16th Sunday in Ordinary Time, Year B • Sacred Heart, Year C • All Souls, 1st Mass *(for alternate response, turn the page)*

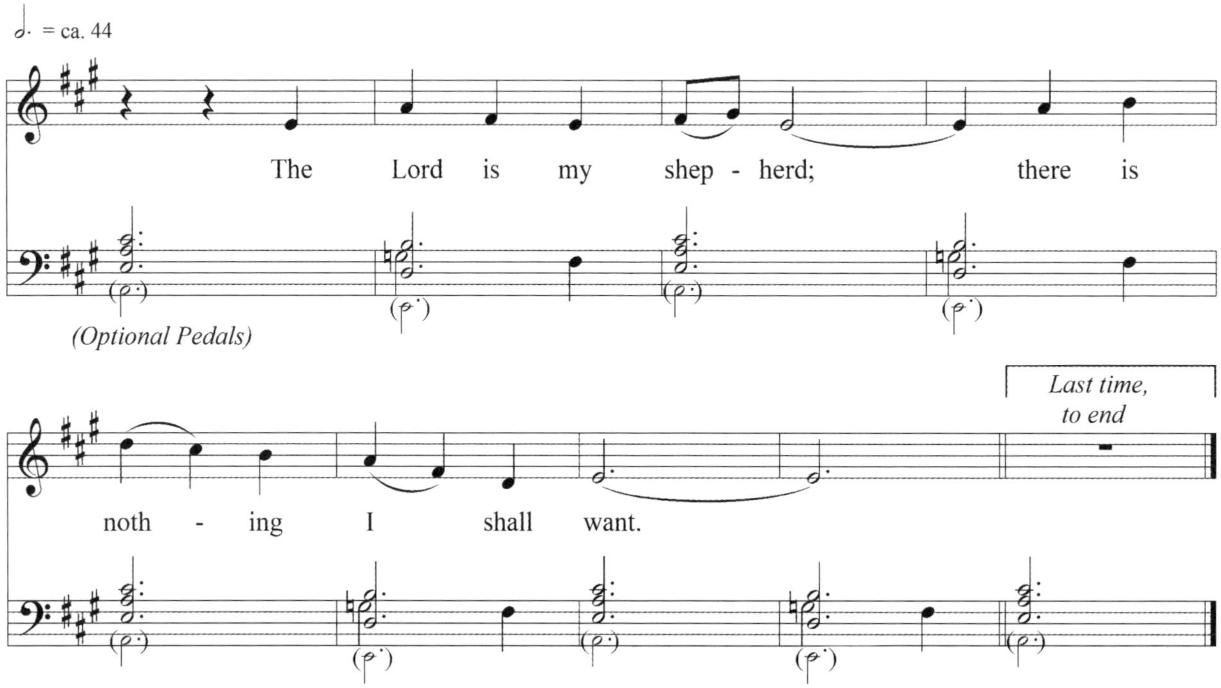

4th Sunday of Easter, Year A, *alternate response*

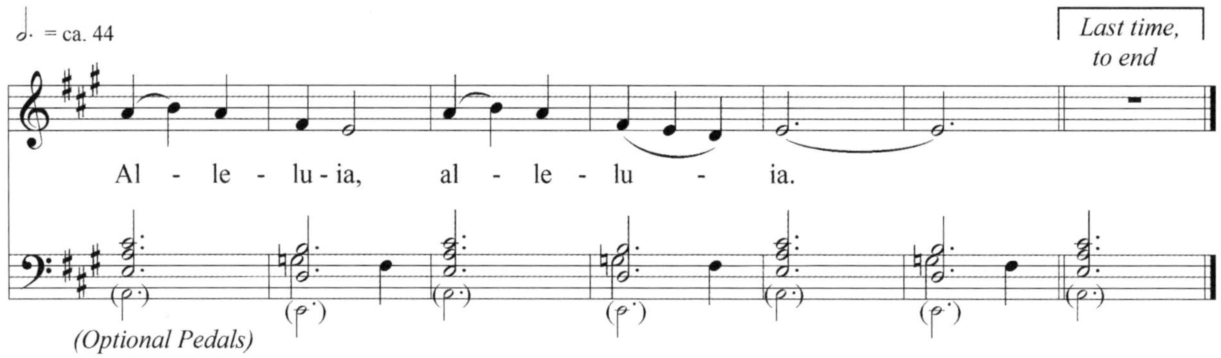

Psalm Tone

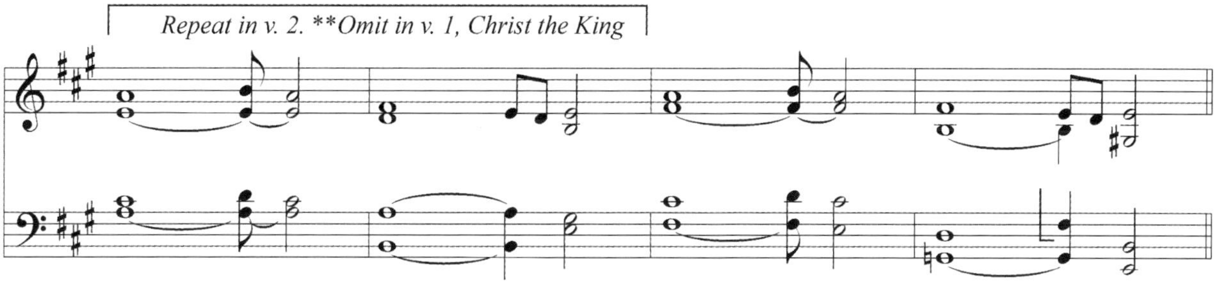

All except Christ the King A
Psalm 23:1-3a, 3b-4, 5, 6. R/ v. 1

1. The LORD is my shepherd; I shall not want.
   In verdant pastures he gives me repose;
   beside restful waters he leads me;
   he refreshes my soul. *R/*

2. He guides me in right paths
   for his name's sake.
   [*Repeat mm. 1-2*]
   Even though I walk in the dark valley
   I fear no evil; for you are at my side
   with your rod and your staff
   that give me courage. *R/*

3. You spread the table before me
   in the sight of my foes;
   you anoint my head with oil;
   my cup overflows. *R/*

4. Only goodness and kindness follow me
   all the days of my life;
   and I shall dwell in the house of the LORD
   for years to come. *R/*

Christ the King A only
Psalm 23:1-2, 2-3, 5-6. R/ v. 1

1. [*Omit mm. 1-2*]
   **The LORD is my shepherd; I shall not want.
   In verdant pastures he gives me repose. *R/*

2. Beside restful waters he leads me;
   he refreshes my soul.
   He guides me in right paths
   for his name's sake. *R/*

3. You spread the table before me
   in the sight of my foes;
   you anoint my head with oil;
   my cup overflows. *R/*

4. Only goodness and kindness follow me
   all the days of my life;
   and I shall dwell in the house of the LORD
   for years to come. *R/*

28th Sunday in Ordinary Time, Year A

All Souls, 1st Mass, *alternate response*

Psalm Tone

Psalm 23:1-3a, 3b-4, 5, 6. R/ v. 4ab

1. The LORD is my shepherd; I shall not want.
In verdant pastures he gives me repose;
beside restful waters he leads me;
he refreshes my soul. *R/*

2. He guides me in right paths
for his name's sake.
[*Repeat mm. 1-2*]
Even though I walk in the dark valley
I fear no evil; for you are at my side
with your rod and your staff
that give me courage. *R/*

3. You spread the table before me
in the sight of my foes;
you anoint my head with oil;
my cup overflows. *R/*

4. Only goodness and kindness follow me
all the days of my life;
and I shall dwell in the house of the LORD
for years to come. *R/*

Psalm 24

4th Sunday of Advent, Year A

Presentation of the Lord

All Saints

Psalm Tone

4 Advent A
All Saints
Psalm 24:1-2, 3-4, 5-6. R/ vv. 7c and 10b; see v. 6

1. The LORD's are the earth and its fullness;
the world and those who dwell in it.
For he founded it upon the seas
and established it upon the rivers. *R/*

2. Who can ascend the mountain of the LORD?
or who may stand in his holy place?
One whose hands are sinless, whose heart is clean,
who desires not what is vain. *R/*

3. He shall receive a blessing from the LORD,
a reward from God his savior.
Such is the race that seeks for him,
that seeks the face of the God of Jacob. *R/*

Presentation
Psalm 24:7, 8, 9, 10. R/ v. 8

1. Lift up, O gates, your lintels;
reach up, you ancient portals,
* that the king of glory may come in! *R/*

2. Who is this king of glory?
The LORD, strong and mighty,
* the LORD, mighty in battle. *R/*

3. Lift up, O gates, your lintels;
reach up, you ancient portals,
* that the king of glory may come in! *R/*

4. Who is this king of glory?
The LORD of hosts;
* he is the king of glory. *R/*

Psalm 25

26th Sunday in Ordinary Time, Year A

All Souls Day, 2nd Mass • 1st Sunday of Advent, Year C • Common Advent 1

All Souls Day, 2nd Mass, *alternate response*

1st Sunday of Lent, Year B

3rd Sunday in Ordinary Time, Year B

Psalm Tone

1 Lent B, 3 OT B
Psalm 25:4-5, 6-7, 8-9. R/ cf. v. 10; v. 4a

1. Your ways, O LORD, make known to me;
teach me your paths,
guide me in your truth and teach me,
for you are God my savior. *R/*

2. Remember that your compassion, O LORD,
and your love are from of old.
In your kindness remember me,
because of your goodness, O LORD. *R/*

3. Good and upright is the LORD;
thus he shows sinners the way.
He guides the humble to justice
and teaches the humble his way. *R/*

26 OT A [1. - 2a. - 3.]

As at left, with R/ v. 6a, and ***v. 2a*** *instead of* ***v. 2***

2a. Remember that your compassion, O LORD,
and your love are from of old.
The sins of my youth and my frailties remember not;
in your kindness remember me,
because of your goodness, O LORD. *R/*

1 Adv C, Common Advent 1 [1. - 3. - 4.]
Psalm 25:4-5, 8-9, 10, 14. R/ v. 1b

vv. 1 and 3 as at left (omit v. 2)

4. All the paths of the LORD are kindness and constancy
toward those who keep his covenant and his decrees.
The friendship of the LORD is with those who fear him,
and his covenant, for their instruction. *R/*

All Souls 2
Psalm 25:6 and 7b, 17-18, 20-21. R/ v. 1a or v. 3a

v. 1 = same as ***v. 2*** *above*

2. Relieve the troubles of my heart;
and bring me out of my distress.
Put an end to my affliction and my suffering;
and take away all my sins. *R/*

3. Preserve my life and rescue me;
let me not be put to shame, for I take refuge in you.
Let integrity and uprightness preserve me,
because I wait for you, O LORD. *R/*

Psalm 27

3rd Sunday in Ordinary Time, Year A • 2nd Sunday of Lent, Year C • All Souls, 3rd Mass • Common Ordinary Time 2

7th Sunday of Easter, Year A • All Souls, 3rd Mass, *alternate response*

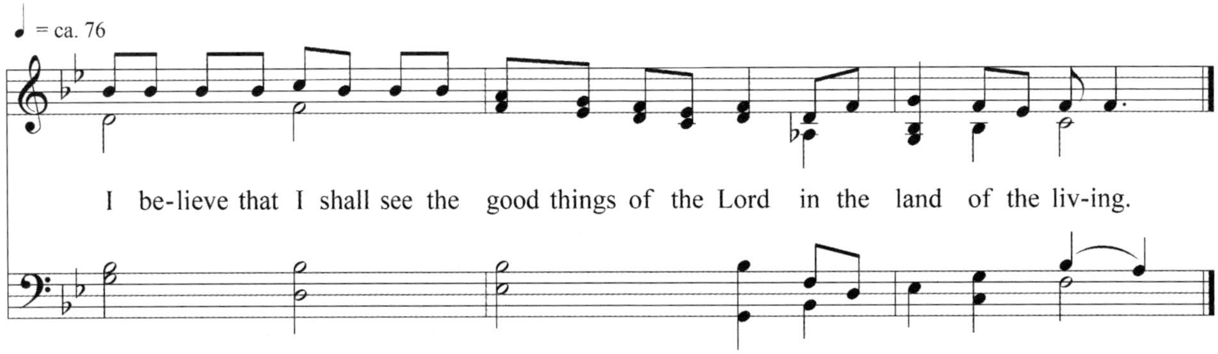

Psalm Tone

Psalm 27:1, 7-8, 8-9, 13-14. R/ v. 1a; 13

7 Easter A
1. - 2. - 3.
3 OT A, Common OT 2
1. - 2. - 5.
2 Lent C
1. - 3. - 4. - 5.
All Souls 3
1. - 2. - 3a. - 5.

1. The LORD is my light and my salvation;
whom___ should I fear?
The LORD is my life's refuge;
of whom should I be afraid? *R/*

Omit on 2 Lent C

2. One thing I ask of the LORD;
this___ I___ seek:
to dwell in the house of the LORD
all the days of my life,
[*Repeat mm. 3-4*]
that I may gaze on the loveliness of the LORD
and contemplate his temple. *R/*

7 Easter A and 2 Lent C only

3. Hear, O LORD, the sound of my call;
have pity on me, and answer me.
Of you my heart speaks;
you my glance__ seeks. *R/*

2 Lent C only

4. Your presence, O LORD, I seek.
Hide not your face from me;
do not in anger repel your servant.
You are my helper: cast me not off. *R/*

Omit on 7 Easter A

5. I believe that I shall see the bounty of the LORD
in the land___ of the living.
Wait for the LORD, with courage;
be stouthearted, and wait for the LORD. *R/*

All Souls 3 only

3a. Hear, O LORD, the sound of my call;
have pity on me, and answer me.
Your presence, O LORD, I seek.
Hide not your face from me. *R/*

Psalm 29

Baptism of the Lord, Year A

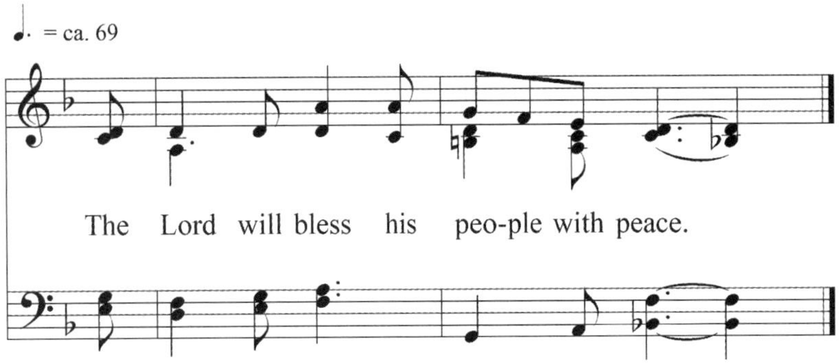

Psalm Tone

Psalm 29:1-2, 3-4, 3, 9-10. R/ v. 11

1. Give to the Lord, you sons of God,
   give to the Lord glory and praise,
   give to the Lord the glory due his name;
   adore the Lord in holy attire. *R/*

2. The voice of the Lord is over the waters,
   the Lord, over vast waters.
   The voice of the Lord is mighty;
   the voice of the Lord is majestic. *R/*

3. The God of glory thunders,
   and in his temple all say, “Glory!”
   The Lord is enthroned above the flood;
   the Lord is enthroned as king forever. *R/*

Psalm 30

Easter Vigil 4 • 13th Sunday in Ordinary Time, Year B • 3rd Sunday of Easter, Year C • 10th Sunday in Ordinary Time, Year C

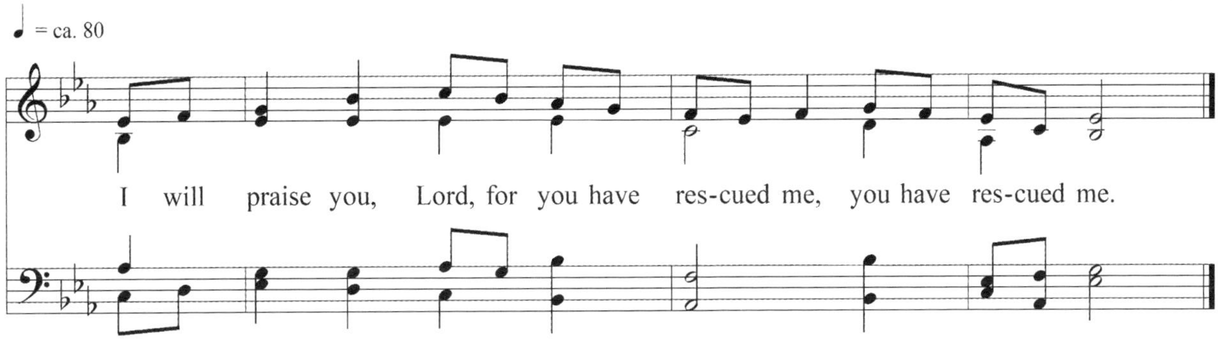

3rd Sunday of Easter, Year C, *alternate response*

Psalm Tone

Psalm 30:2, 4, 5-6, 11-12, 13. R/ v. 2a

1. I will extol you, O LORD, for you drew me clear
and did not let my enemies rejoice over me.
O LORD, you brought me up from the netherworld;
you preserved me from among those
going down into the pit. *R/*

2. Sing praise to the LORD, you his faithful ones,
and give thanks to his holy name.
For his anger lasts but a moment;
a lifetime, his good will.
At nightfall, weeping enters in,
but with the dawn, rejoicing. *R/*

3. Hear, O LORD, and have pity on me;
O LORD, be my helper.
You changed my mourning into dancing;
O LORD, my God, forever will I give you thanks. *R/*

Psalm 31

Good Friday

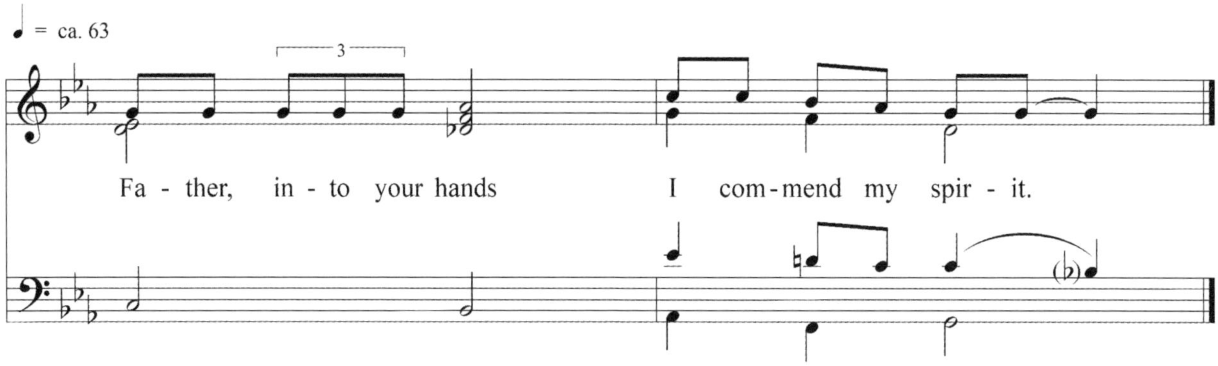

Psalm Tone

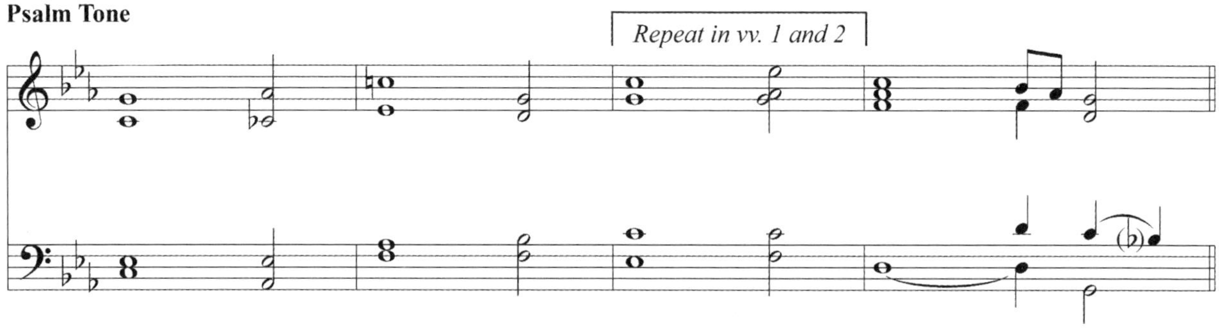

Psalm 31:2, 6, 12-13, 15-16, 17, 25. R/ Lk 23:46

1. In you, O Lord, I take refuge;
   let me never be put to shame.
   In your justice rescue me.
   [*Repeat m. 3*]
   Into your hands I commend my spirit;
   you will redeem me, O Lord, O faithful God. *R/*

2. For all my foes I am an object of reproach,
   a laughingstock to my neighbors, and a dread to my friends;
   they who see me abroad flee from me.
   [*Repeat m. 3*]
   I am forgotten like the unremembered dead;
   I am like a dish that is broken. *R/*

3. But my trust is in you, O Lord;
   I say, "You are my God.
   In your hands is my destiny; rescue me
   from the clutches of my enemies and my persecutors." *R/*

4. Let your face shine upon your servant;
   save me in your kindness.
   Take courage and be stouthearted,
   all you who hope in the Lord. *R/*

9th Sunday in Ordinary Time, Year A

Psalm Tone

Psalm 31:2-3, 3-4, 17, 25. R/ v. 3b

1. In you, O Lord, I take refuge;
   let me never be put to shame.
   In your justice rescue me,
   [*Repeat m. 3*]
   incline your ear to me,
   make haste to deliver me! *R/*

2. Be my rock of refuge,
   a stronghold to give me safety.
   You are my rock and my fortress;
   for your name's sake you will lead and guide me. *R/*

3. Let your face shine upon your servant;
   save me in your kindness.
   Take courage and be stouthearted,
   all you who hope in the Lord. *R/*

Psalm 32

6th Sunday in Ordinary Time, Year B

11th Sunday in Ordinary Time, Year C

Psalm 32:1-2, 5, 7, 11. R/ v. 7, cf. v. 5c

6 OT B only

1. Blessed is he whose fault is taken away,
   whose sin is covered.
   Blessed the man to whom the LORD imputes not guilt,
   in whose spirit there is no guile. *R/*

11 OT C only

1a. Blessed is the one whose fault is taken away,
   whose sin is covered.
   Blessed the man to who the LORD imputes
   not guilt,
   in whose spirit there is no guile. *R/*

2. I acknowledged my sin to you,
   my guilt I covered not.
   I said, "I confess my faults to the LORD,"
   and you took away the guilt of my sin. *R/*

11 OT C only

3. You are my shelter;
   from distress you will preserve me;
   with glad cries of freedom
   you will ring me round. *R/*

4. ** Be glad in the LORD and rejoice, you just;
   exult, all you upright of heart. *R/*

6 OT B	**11 OT C**
1. - 2. - 4	1a. - 2. - 3. - 4.

Psalm 32

6th Sunday in Ordinary Time, Year B

11th Sunday in Ordinary Time, Year C

Psalm Tone

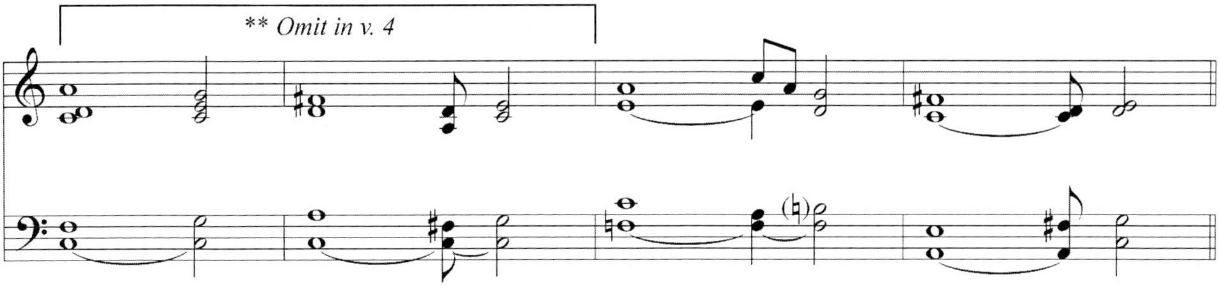

Psalm 32:1-2, 5, 7, 11. R/ v. 7, cf. v. 5c

6 OT B only

1. Blessed is he whose fault is taken away,
 whose sin is covered.
 Blessed the man to whom the LORD imputes not guilt,
 in whose spirit there is no guile. *R/*

2. Then I acknowledged my sin to you,
 my guilt I covered not.
 I said, "I confess my faults to the LORD,"
 and you took away the guilt of my sin. *R/*

11 OT C only

1a. Blessed is the one whose fault is taken away,
 whose sin is covered.
 Blessed the man to who the LORD imputes not guilt,
 in whose spirit there is no guile. *R/*

2a. I acknowledged my sin to you,
 my guilt I covered not.
 I said, "I confess my faults to the LORD,"
 and you took away the guilt of my sin. *R/*

3. You are my shelter;
 from distress you will preserve me;
 with glad cries of freedom
 you will ring me round. *R/*

4. ** Be glad in the LORD and rejoice, you just;
 exult, all you upright of heart. *R/*

6 OT B	11 OT C
1. - 2. - 4	1a. - 2a. - 3. - 4.

Psalm 33

2nd Sunday of Lent, Year A • 5th Sunday of Easter, Year A •
29th Sunday in Ordinary Time, Year B

Pentecost Vigil 1 • Trinity Sunday, Year B • 19th Sunday in Ordinary Time, Year C

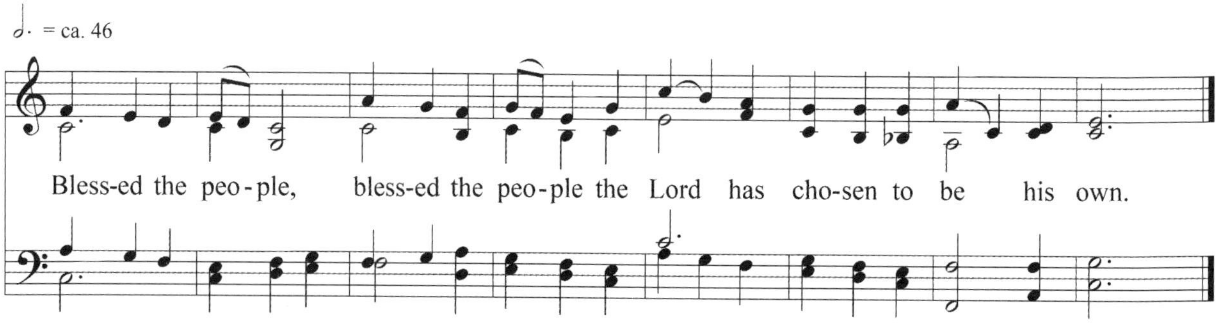

Easter Vigil 1, *alternate psalm*

5th Sunday of Easter, Year A, *alternate response*

Psalm Tone

Psalm 33:1-2, 4-5, 6, 7, 8- 9, 10-11, 12-13, 14-15, 18-19, 20, 22. R/ v. 22; 12b; 5b

5 Easter A, 19 OT C

1. Exult, you just, in the LORD;
praise from the upright is fitting.
Give thanks to the LORD on the harp;
with the ten–stringed lyre chant his praises. *R/*

Easter Vigil 1, alt., 2 Lent A, 5 Easter A, Trinity B, 29 OT B

2. Upright is the word of the LORD,
and all his works are trustworthy.
He loves justice and right;
of the kindness of the LORD the earth is full. *R/*

Easter Vigil 1, alt.

3. By the word of the LORD the heavens were made;
by the breath of his mouth all their host.
He gathers the waters of the sea as in a flask;
in cellars he confines the deep. *R/*

2 Lent A, 5 Easter A, Trinity B, 29 OT B, 19 OT C

4. See, the eyes of the LORD are upon those who fear him,
upon those who hope for his kindness,
to deliver them from death
and preserve them in spite of famine. *R/*

Easter Vigil 1, alt., 2 Lent A, Trinity B, 29 OT B, 19 OT C

5. Our soul waits for the LORD,
who is our help and our shield.
May your kindness, O LORD, be upon us
who have put our hope in you. *R/*

Pentecost Vigil

1a. The LORD brings to nought the plans of nations;
he foils the designs of peoples.
But the plan of the LORD stands forever;
the design of his heart, through all generations. *R/*

Trinity B

3a. By the word of the LORD the heavens were made;
by the breath of his mouth all their host.
For he spoke, and it was made;
he commanded, and it stood forth. *R/*

Easter Vigil 1, alt., Pentecost Vigil

4a. Blessed the nation whose God is the LORD,
the people he has chosen for his own inheritance.
From heaven the LORD looks down;
he sees all mankind. *R/*

Pentecost Vigil

5a. From his fixed throne he beholds
all who dwell on the earth,
He who fashioned the heart of each,
he who knows all their works. *R/*

2 Lent A, 29 OT B 2. - 4. - 5.	**Pentecost Vigil** 1a. - 4a. - 5a.
Easter Vigil 1, alt. 2. - 3. - 4a. - 5.	**Trinity B** 2. - 3a. - 4. - 5.
5 Easter A 1. - 2. - 4. - 5.	**19 OT C** 1. - 4. - 5.

Psalm 34

19th, 20th, and 21st Sunday in Ordinary Time, Year B • 4th Sunday of Lent, Year C • Common Ordinary Time 3, *alternate response*

Common Ordinary Time 3

Saints Peter and Paul, Day Mass

30th Sunday in Ordinary Time, Year C

Psalm Tone

Psalm 34:2-3, 4-5, 6-7, 8-9, 16-17, 18-19, 20-21, 23. R/ vv. 9a; 2; 8b; 7a

1. I will bless the LORD at all times;
   his praise shall be ever in my mouth.
   Let my soul glory in the LORD;
   the lowly will hear me and be glad. *R/*

2. Glorify the LORD with me,
   let us together extol his name.
   I sought the LORD, and he answered me
   and delivered me from all my fears. *R/*

3. Look to him that you may be radiant with joy,
   and your faces may not blush with shame.
   When the afflicted man called out, the LORD heard,
   and from all his distress he saved him. *R/*

Omit on 4 Lent C, 20 OT B

4. The angel of the LORD encamps
   around those who fear him and delivers them.
   Taste and see how good the LORD is;
   blessed the man who takes refuge in him. *R/*

Peter and Paul Day, 19 OT B, Common OT 3
1. - 2. - 3. - 4.

20 OT B
1. - 2. - 3a.

21 OT B
1. - 2b. - 3b. - 4b.

30 OT C
1. - 2c - 3c.

4 Lent C
1. - 2. - 3.

20 OTB only

3a. Look to him that you may be radiant with joy,
and your faces may not blush with shame.
When the poor one called out, the LORD heard,
and from all his distress he saved him. *R/*

21 OT B only

2b. The LORD has eyes for the just,
and ears for their cry.
The LORD confronts the evildoers,
to destroy remembrance of them
from the earth. *R/*

3b. When the just cry out, the LORD hears them,
and from all their distress he rescues them.
The LORD is close to the brokenhearted;
and those who are crushed in spirit he saves. *R/*

4b. Many are the troubles of the just one,
but out of them all the LORD delivers him;
he watches over all his bones;
not one of them shall be broken. *R/*

30 OT C only

2c. The LORD confronts the evildoers,
to destroy remembrance of them from the earth.
When the just cry out, the LORD hears them,
and from all their distress he rescues them. *R/*

3c. The LORD is close to the brokenhearted;
and those who are crushed in spirit he saves.
The LORD redeems the lives of his servants;
no one incurs guilt who takes refuge in him. *R/*

Psalm 40

2nd Sunday in Ordinary Time, Year A • 2nd Sunday in Ordinary Time, Year B • Annunciation

Psalm Tone

Psalm 40:2, 4, 7-8, 8-9, 10. R/ vv. 8a and 9a

2 OT A, 2 OT B 1. - 2. - 3. - 4.
Annunciation 2. - 3. - 4. - 5.

2 OT A and 2 OT B only

1. I have waited, waited for the LORD,
 and he stooped toward me and heard my cry.
 And he put a new song into my mouth,
 a hymn to our God. *R/*

2. Sacrifice or offering you wished not,
 but ears open to obedience you gave me.
 Holocausts or sin-offerings you sought not;
 then said I, "Behold I come." *R/*

3. "In the written scroll it is prescribed for me,
 to do your will, O my God, is my delight,
 * and your law is within my heart!" *R/*

4. ** I announced your justice in the vast assembly;
 I did not restrain my lips, as you, O LORD, know. *R/*

Annunciation only

5. Your justice I kept not hid within my heart;
 your faithfulness and your salvation I have spoken of;
 I have made no secret of your kindness and your truth
 in the vast assembly. *R/*

20th Sunday in Ordinary Time, Year C

Psalm Tone

Psalm 40:2, 3, 4, 18. R/ v. 14b

1. ** I have waited, waited for the LORD,
   and he stooped toward me. *R/*

2. The LORD heard my cry.
   He drew me out of the pit of destruction, out of the mud of the swamp;
   he set my feet upon a crag;
   he made firm my steps. *R/*

3. And he put a new song into my mouth,
   a hymn to our God.
   Many shall look on in awe
   and trust in the LORD. *R/*

4. Though I am afflicted and poor,
   yet the LORD thinks of me.
   You are my help and my deliverer;
   O my God, hold not back! *R/*

Psalm 41

7th Sunday in Ordinary Time, Year B

Psalm Tone

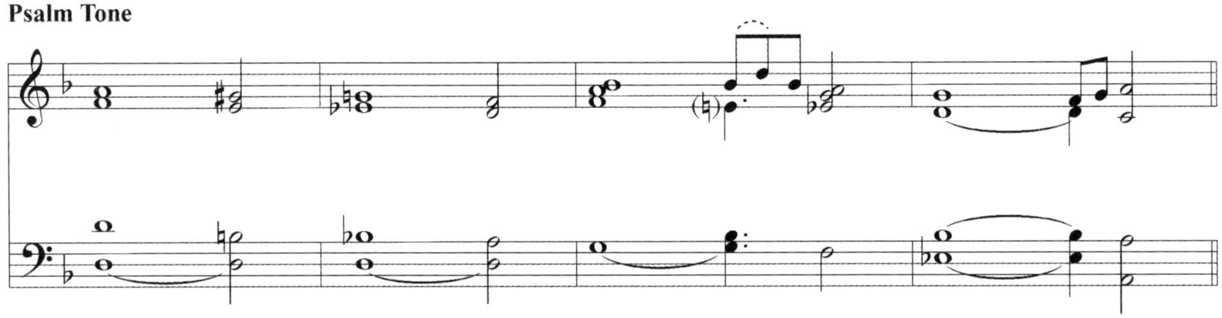

Psalm 41:2-3, 4-5, 13-14. R/ v. 5b

1. Blessed is the one who has regard for the lowly and the poor;
   in the day of misfortune the Lord will deliver him.
   The Lord will keep and preserve him;
   and make him blessed on earth,
   and not give him over to the will of his enemies. *R/*

2. The Lord will help him on his sickbed,
   he will take away all his ailment when he is ill.
   Once I said, "O Lord, have pity on me;
   heal me, though I have sinned against you." *R/*

3. But because of my integrity you sustain me
   and let me stand before you forever.
   Blessed be the Lord, the God of Israel,
   from all eternity. Amen. Amen. *R/*

Psalm 42–43

Easter Vigil 7

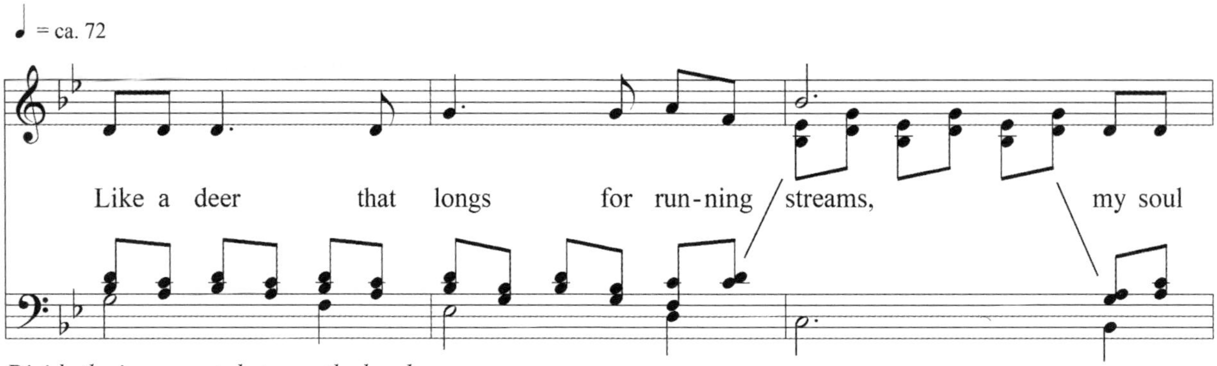

Divide the inner parts between the hands, as necessary.

Psalm Tone

Psalm 42:3, 5; 43:3, 4. R/ 42:2

1. Athirst is my soul
   for God, the living God.
   When shall I go
   and behold the face of God? *R/*

2. I went with the throng
   and led them in procession to the house of God,
   amid loud cries of joy and thanksgiving,
   with the multitude keeping festival. *R/*

3. Send forth your light and your fidelity;
   they shall lead me on
   and bring me to your holy mountain,
   to your dwelling-place. *R/*

4. Then will I go in to the altar of God,
   the God of my gladness and joy;
   then will I give you thanks upon the harp,
   O God, my God! *R/*

Psalm 45

Assumption, Day Mass

Psalm Tone

Psalm 45:10bc, 11, 12ab, 16. R/ v. 10bc

1. The queen takes her place at your right hand
   in gold of Ophir. *R/*

2. Hear, O daughter, and see; turn your ear,
   forget your people and your father's house. *R/*

3. So shall the king desire your beauty;
   for he is your lord. *R/*

4. They are borne in with gladness and joy;
   they enter the palace of the king. *R/*

Psalm 46

Dedication of the Lateran Basilica • Anniversary of the Dedication of a Church, 2nd option

* *Lectionary wording of the response for the Anniversary of Dedication. The wording for the Lateran Basilica seems preferable.*

Psalm Tone

Psalm 46:2-3, 5-6, 8-9. R/ v. 5

1. God is our refuge and our strength,
   an ever-present help in distress.
   Therefore, we fear not, though the earth be shaken
   and mountains plunge into the depths of the sea. *R/*

2. There is a stream whose runlets gladden the city of God,
   the holy dwelling of the Most High.
   God is in its midst; it shall not be disturbed;
   God will help it at the break of dawn. *R/*

3. The Lord of hosts is with us;
   our stronghold is the God of Jacob.
   Come! behold the deeds of the Lord,
   the astounding things he has wrought on earth. *R/*

Psalm 47

Ascension Vigil and Day • Common Ascension

Ascension Vigil and Day, *alternate response*

Psalm Tone

Psalm 47:2-3, 6-7, 8-9. R/ v. 6

1. All you peoples, clap your hands,
   shout to God with cries of gladness,
   for the LORD, the Most High, the awesome,
   is the great king over all the earth. *R/*

2. God mounts his throne amid shouts of joy;
   the LORD, amid trumpet blasts.
   Sing praise to God, sing praise;
   sing praise to our king, sing praise. *R/*

3. For king of all the earth is God;
   sing hymns of praise.
   God reigns over the nations,
   God sits upon his holy throne. *R/*

Psalm 50

10th Sunday in Ordinary Time, Year A

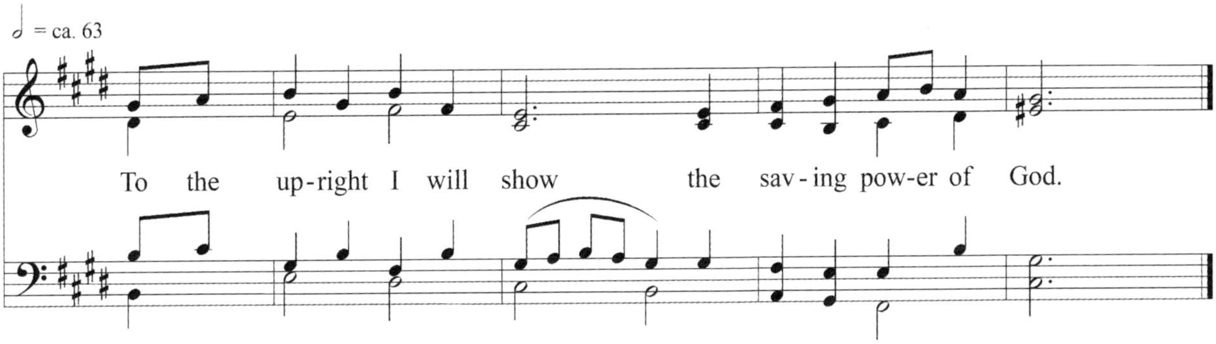

Psalm Tone

Psalm 50:1, 8, 12-13, 14-15. R/ v. 23b

1. God the LORD has spoken and summoned the earth,
 from the rising of the sun to its setting.
 "Not for your sacrifices do I rebuke you,
 for your holocausts are before me always." *R/*

2. "If I were hungry, I would not tell you,
 for mine are the world and its fullness.
 Do I eat the flesh of strong bulls,
 or is the blood of goats my drink?" *R/*

3. "Offer to God praise as your sacrifice
 and fulfill your vows to the Most High;
 then call upon me in time of distress;
 I will rescue you, and you shall glorify me." *R/*

Psalm 51

Ash Wednesday • 1st Sunday in Lent, Year A • Common Lent 1

5th Sunday of Lent, Year B • Easter Vigil 7, *alternate psalm*

24th Sunday in Ordinary Time, Year C

Psalm Tone

Psalm 51:3-4, 5-6ab, 12-13, 14, 17, 18-19. R/ see v. 3a; 12a; Lk 15:18

1. Have mercy on me, God, in your goodness;
 in the greatness of your compassion wipe out my offense.
 Thoroughly wash me from my guilt;
 and of my sin cleanse me. *R/*

Omit on Easter Vigil 7, alt., 5 Lent B, 24 OTC

2. For I acknowledge my offense,
 and my sin is before me always.
 "Against you only have I sinned,
 and done what is evil in your sight." *R/*

Omit on Easter Vigil 7, alt.,

3. A clean heart create for me, O God;
 and a steadfast spirit renew within me.
 Cast me not out from your presence,
 and your holy spirit take not from me. *R/*

Omit on 24 OT C

4. Give me back the joy of your salvation,
 and a willing spirit sustain in me.
 O Lord, open my lips,
 and my mouth shall proclaim your praise. *R/*

Ash Wednesday, 1 Lent A, Common Lent 1
1. - 2. - 3. - 4.
Easter Vigil 7, alt.
1. - 4. - 5.
5 Lent B
1. - 3. - 4a.
24 OT C
1. - 3. - 5a.

5 Lent B only

4a. Give me back the joy of your salvation,
 and a willing spirit sustain in me.
 I will teach transgressors your ways,
 and sinners shall return to you. *R/*

Easter Vigil 7, alt., only

5. For you are not pleased with sacrifices;
 should I offer a holocaust, you would not accept it.
 My sacrifice, O God, is a contrite spirit;
 a heart contrite and humbled, O God, you will not spurn. *R/*

24 OT C only

5a. O Lord, open my lips,
 and my mouth shall proclaim your praise.
 My sacrifice, O God, is a contrite spirit;
 a heart contrite and humbled, O God, you will not spurn. *R/*

Psalm 54

25th Sunday in Ordinary Time, Year B

Psalm Tone

Psalm 54:3-4, 5, 6-8. R/ v. 6b

1. O God, by your name save me,
   and by your might defend my cause.
   O God, hear my prayer;
   hearken to the words of my mouth. *R/*

2. For the haughty men have risen up against me,
   the ruthless seek my life;
   * they set not God before their eyes. *R/*

3. Behold, God is my helper;
   the Lord sustains my life.
   Freely will I offer you sacrifice;
   I will praise your name, O LORD, for its goodness. *R/*

Psalm 62

8th Sunday in Ordinary Time, Year A

Psalm Tone

Psalm 62:2-3, 6-7, 8-9. R/ v. 6a

1. Only in God is my soul at rest;
   from him comes my salvation.
   He only is my rock and my salvation,
   my stronghold; I shall not be disturbed at all. *R/*

2. Only in God be at rest, my soul,
   for from him comes my hope.
   He only is my rock and my salvation,
   my stronghold; I shall not be disturbed. *R/*

3. With God is my safety and my glory,
   he is the rock of my strength; my refuge is in God.
   Trust in him at all times, O my people!
   Pour out your hearts before him. *R/*

Psalm 63

22nd Sunday in Ordinary Time, Year A • 32nd Sunday in Ordinary Time, Year A • 12th Sunday in Ordinary Time, Year C • Common Ordinary Time 4

The response may be sung twice after each verse

Psalm Tone

Psalm 63:2, 3-4, 5-6, 7, 8-9. R/ v. 2b

1. O God, you are my God whom I seek;
   for you my flesh pines and my soul thirsts
   * like the earth, parched, lifeless and without water. *R/*

2. Thus have I gazed toward you in the sanctuary
   to see your power and your glory,
   for your kindness is a greater good than life;
   my lips shall glorify you. *R/*

3. Thus will I bless you while I live;
   lifting up my hands, I will call upon your name.
   As with the riches of a banquet shall my soul be satisfied,
   and with exultant lips my mouth shall praise you. *R/*

Note:
There are very minor differences of wording in ***Common OT 4*** in v. 1, line 3, and v. 3, line 1.

22 OT A, 12 OT C, Common OT 4 only

4. You are my help,
   and in the shadow of your wings I shout for joy.
   My soul clings fast to you;
   your right hand upholds me. *R/*

32 OT A only

4a. I will remember you upon my couch,
    and through the night-watches I will meditate on you:
    you are my help,
    and in the shadow of your wings I shout for joy. *R/*

Psalm 65

15th Sunday in Ordinary Time, Year A

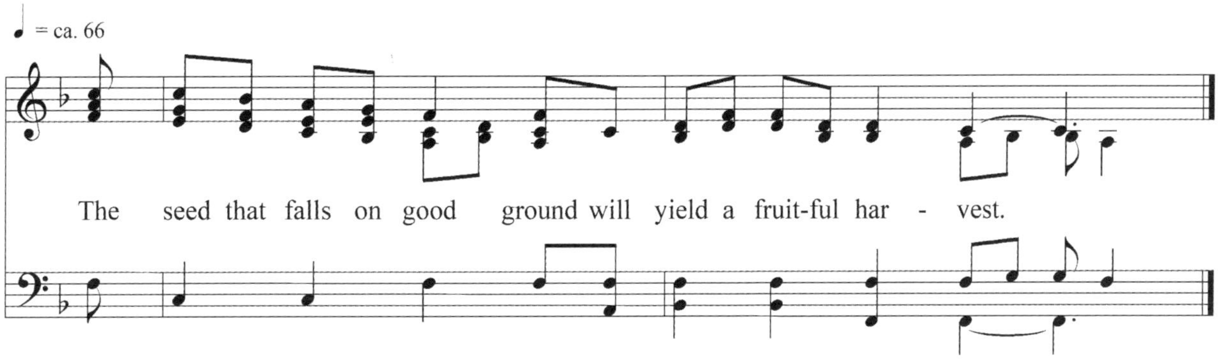

Psalm Tone

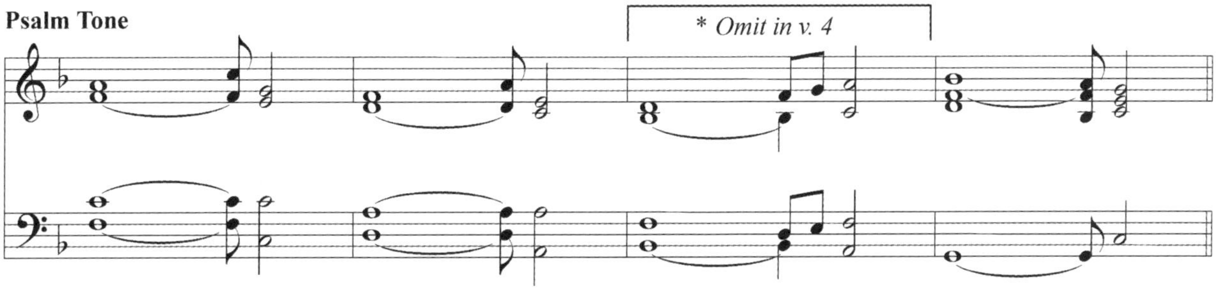

Psalm 65:10, 11, 12-13, 14. R/ Lk 8:8

1. You have visited the land and watered it;
   greatly have you enriched it.
   God's watercourses are filled;
   you have prepared the grain. *R/*

2. Thus have you prepared the land: drenching its furrows,
   breaking up its clods,
   softening it with showers,
   blessing its yield. *R/*

3. You have crowned the year with your bounty,
   and your paths overflow with a rich harvest;
   the untilled meadows overflow with it,
   and rejoicing clothes the hills. *R/*

4. The fields are garmented with flocks
   and the valleys blanketed with grain.
   * They shout and sing for joy. *R/*

Psalm 66

6th Sunday of Easter, Year A • 14th Sunday in Ordinary Time, Year C

6th Sunday of Easter, *alternate response*

Common Eastertide 2

Psalm Tone

Psalm 66:1-3, 4-5, 6-7, 16, 20. R/ v. 1

1. Shout joyfully to God, all the earth,
   sing praise to the glory of his name;
   proclaim his glorious praise.
   Say to God, "How tremendous are your deeds!" *R/*

2. "Let all on earth worship and sing praise to you,
   sing praise to your name!"
   Come and see the works of God,
   his tremendous deeds among the children of Adam. *R/*

3. He has changed the sea into dry land;
   through the river they passed on foot.
   Therefore let us rejoice in him.
   He rules by his might forever. *R/*

4. Hear now, all you who fear God,
   while I declare what he has done for me.
   Blessed be God who refused me not
   my prayer or his kindness! *R/*

Psalm 67

Mary, the Mother of God (January 1)

20th Sunday in Ordinary Time, Year A • 6th Sunday of Easter, Year C • Thanksgiving Day, *C.E. alternate psalm, alternate response*

Thanksgiving Day, *C.E. alternate psalm*

Psalm Tone

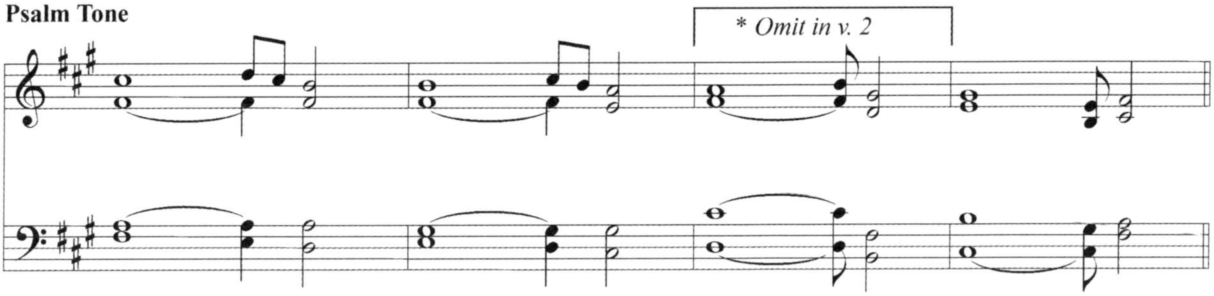

Psalm 67:2-3, 5, 6, 8 R/ v. 2a; v. 4; v. 7

1. May God have pity on us and bless us;
   may he let his face shine upon us.
   So may your way be known upon earth;
   among all nations, your salvation. *R/*

2. May the nations be glad and exult
   because you rule the peoples in equity;
   * the nations on the earth you guide. *R/*

3. May the peoples praise you, O God;
   may all the peoples praise you!
   May God bless us,
   and may all the ends of the earth fear him! *R/*

Psalm 68

22nd Sunday in Ordinary Time, Year C

Psalm Tone

Psalm 68:4-5, 6-7, 10-11. R/ see v. 11b

1. The just rejoice and exult before God;
   they are glad and rejoice.
   Sing to God, chant praise to his name;
   whose name is the LORD. *R/*

2. The father of orphans and the defender of widows
   is God in his holy dwelling.
   God gives a home to the forsaken;
   he leads forth prisoners to prosperity. *R/*

3. A bountiful rain you showered down, O God, upon your inheritance;
   you restored the land when it languished;
   your flock settled in it;
   in your goodness, O God, you provided it for the needy. *R/*

Psalm 69

12th Sunday in Ordinary Time, Year A

Psalm Tone

Psalm 69:8-10, 14, 17, 33-35. R/ v. 14c

1. For your sake I bear insult,
   and shame covers my face.
   I have become an outcast to my brothers,
   a stranger to my children,
   because zeal for your house consumes me,
   and the insults of those who blaspheme you fall upon me. *R/*

2. I pray to you, O Lord,
   for the time of your favor, O God!
   In your great kindness answer me
   with your constant help.
   Answer me, O Lord, for bounteous is your kindness;
   in your great mercy turn toward me. *R/*

3. "See, you lowly ones, and be glad;
   you who seek God, may your hearts revive!
   For the Lord hears the poor,
   and his own who are in bonds he spurns not.
   Let the heavens and the earth praise him,
   the seas and whatever moves in them!" *R/*

15th Sunday in Ordinary Time, Year C

Psalm Tone

Psalm 69:14, 17, 30-31, 33-34, 36, 37. R/ see v. 33

1. I pray to you, O LORD,
   for the time of your favor, O God!
   In your great kindness answer me
   with your constant help.
   Answer me, O LORD, for bounteous is your kindness:
   in your great mercy turn toward me. *R/*

2. I am afflicted and in pain;
   let your saving help, O God, protect me.
   I will praise the name of God in song,
   and I will glorify him with thanksgiving. *R/*

3. "See, you lowly ones, and be glad;
   you who seek God, may your hearts revive!
   For the LORD hears the poor,
   and his own who are in bonds he spurns not." *R/*

4. For God will save Zion
   and rebuild the cities of Judah.
   The descendants of his servants shall inherit it,
   and those who love his name shall inhabit it. *R/*

Psalm 71

4th Sunday in Ordinary Time, Year C

St. John the Baptist, Vigil Mass

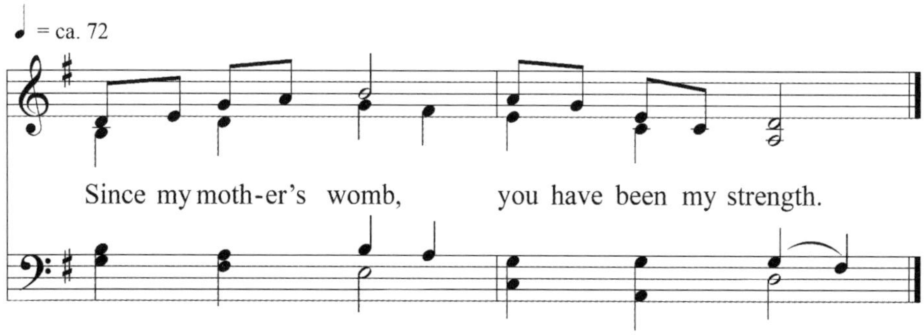

Psalm Tone

Psalm 71:1-2, 3-4, 5-6, 15, 17. R/ see v. 15ab; v. 6

1. In you, O LORD, I take refuge;
   let me never be put to shame.
   In your justice rescue me, and deliver me;
   incline your ear to me, and save me. *R/*

2. Be my rock of refuge,
   a stronghold to give me safety,
   for you are my rock and my fortress.
   O my God, rescue me from the hand of the wicked. *R/*

3. For you are my hope, O Lord;
   my trust, O God, from my youth.
   On you I depend from birth;
   from my mother's womb you are my strength. *R/*

4. My mouth shall declare your justice,
   day by day your salvation.
   O God, you have taught me from my youth,
   and till the present I proclaim your wondrous deeds. *R/*

Psalm 72

Epiphany of the Lord, Vigil and Day • Common Epiphany

Epiphany
1. - 2. - 3. - 4.
2 Advent A
1. - 2. - 4. - 5.

2nd Sunday of Advent, Year A

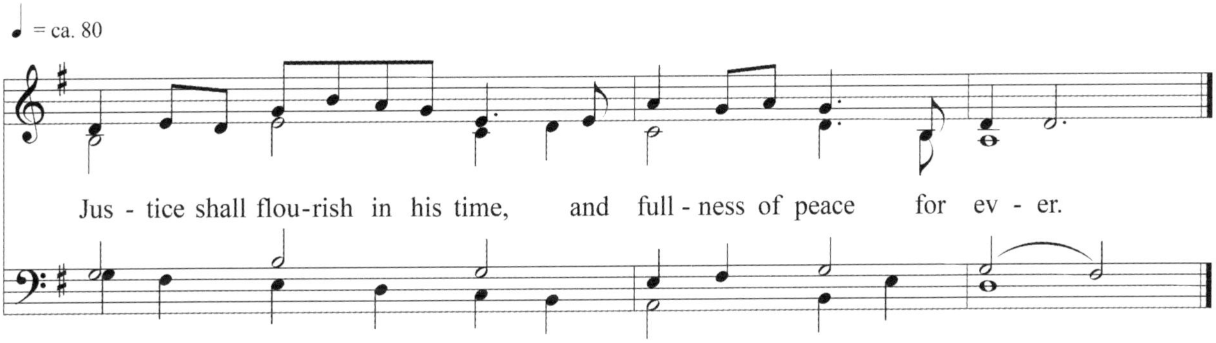

Psalm Tone

Psalm 72:1-2, 7-8, 10-11, 12-13, 17. R/ cf. v. 11; cf. v. 7

1. O God, with your judgment endow the king,
and with your justice the king's son;
he shall govern your people with justice
and your afflicted ones with judgment. *R/*

2. Justice shall flower in his days,
and profound peace, till the moon be no more.
May he rule from sea to sea,
and from the River to the ends of the earth. *R/*

Epiphany and Common Epiphany only:

3. The kings of Tarshish and the Isles shall offer gifts;
the kings of Arabia and Seba shall bring tribute.
All kings shall pay him homage,
all nations shall serve him. *R/*

4. For he shall rescue the poor when he cries out,
and the afflicted when he has no one to help him.
He shall have pity for the lowly and the poor;
the lives of the poor he shall save. *R/*

2 Advent A only:

5. May his name be blessed forever;
as long as the sun his name shall remain.
In him shall all the tribes of the earth be blessed;
all the nations shall proclaim his happiness. *R/*

Psalm 78

18th Sunday in Ordinary Time, Year B

Psalm Tone

Psalm 78:3-4, 23-24, 25, 54. R/ v. 24b

1. What we have heard and know,
   and what our fathers have declared to us,
   we will declare to the generation to come
   the glorious deeds of the LORD and his strength
   [*Repeat m. 4*]
   and the wonders that he wrought. *R/*

2. He commanded the skies above
   and opened the doors of heaven;
   he rained manna upon them for food
   and gave them heavenly bread. *R/*

3. Man ate the bread of angels,
   food he sent them in abundance.
   And he brought them to his holy land,
   to the mountains his right hand had won. *R/*

Exaltation of the Holy Cross

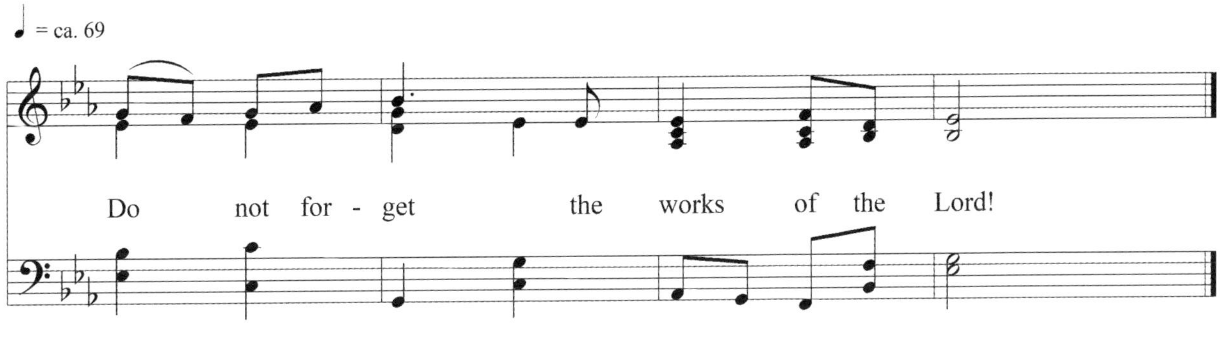

Psalm Tone

Psalm 78:1bc-2, 34-35, 36-37, 38. R/ see v. 7b

1. Hearken, my people, to my teaching;
   incline your ears to the words of my mouth.
   I will open my mouth in a parable,
   I will utter mysteries from of old. *R/*

2. While he slew them they sought him
   and inquired after God again,
   Remembering that God was their rock
   and the Most High God, their redeemer *R/*

3. But they flattered him with their mouths
   and lied to him with their tongues,
   Though their hearts were not steadfast toward him,
   nor were they faithful to his covenant. *R/*

4. But he, being merciful, forgave their sin
   and destroyed them not;
   Often he turned back his anger
   and let none of his wrath be roused. *R/*

Psalm 80

1st Sunday of Advent, Year B • 4th Sunday of Advent, Year C

Psalm Tone

Psalm 80:2-3, 15-16, 18-19 R/ v. 4

1. O shepherd of Israel, hearken,
   from your throne upon the cherubim, shine forth.
   Rouse your power,
   and come to save us. *R/*

2. Once again, O Lord of hosts,
   look down from heaven, and see;
   take care of this vine,
       and protect what your right hand has planted,
   the son of man whom you yourself made strong. *R/*

3. May your help be with the man of your right hand,
   with the son of man whom you yourself made strong.
   Then we will no more withdraw from you;
   give us new life, and we will call upon your name. *R/*

27th Sunday in Ordinary Time, Year A

Psalm Tone

Psalm 80:9, 12, 13-14, 15-16, 19-20 R/ Isaiah 5:7a

1. A vine from Egypt you transplanted;
   you drove away the nations and planted it.
   It put forth its foliage to the Sea,
   its shoots as far as the River. *R/*

2. Why have you broken down its walls,
   so that every passer-by plucks its fruit,
   the boar from the forest lays it waste,
   and the beasts of the field feed upon it? *R/*

3. Once again, O Lord of hosts,
   look down from heaven, and see;
   take care of this vine,
   and protect what your right hand has planted
   the son of man whom you yourself made strong. *R/*

4. Then we will no more withdraw from you;
   give us new life, and we will call upon your name.
   O Lord, God of hosts, restore us;
   if your face shine upon us, then we shall be saved. *R/*

Psalm 81

9th Sunday in Ordinary Time, Year B

Psalm Tone

Psalm 81:3-4, 5-6, 7-8, 10-11. R/ v. 2a

1. Take up a melody, and sound the timbrel,
   the pleasant harp and the lyre.
   Blow the trumpet at the new moon,
   at the full moon, on our solemn feast. *R/*

2. For it is a statute in Israel,
   an ordinance of the God of Jacob,
   who made it a decree for Joseph
   when he came forth from the land of Egypt. *R/*

3. An unfamiliar speech I hear:
   "I relieved his shoulder of the burden;
   his hands were freed from the basket.
   In distress you called, and I rescued you." *R/*

4. "There shall be no strange god among you
   nor shall you worship any alien god.
   I, the LORD, am your God
   who led you forth from the land of Egypt." *R/*

Psalm 84

Holy Family, Year C option

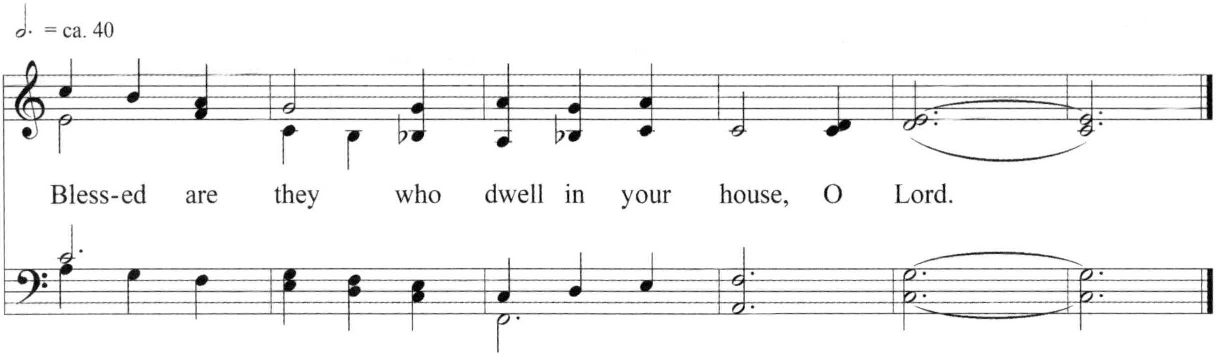

Psalm Tone

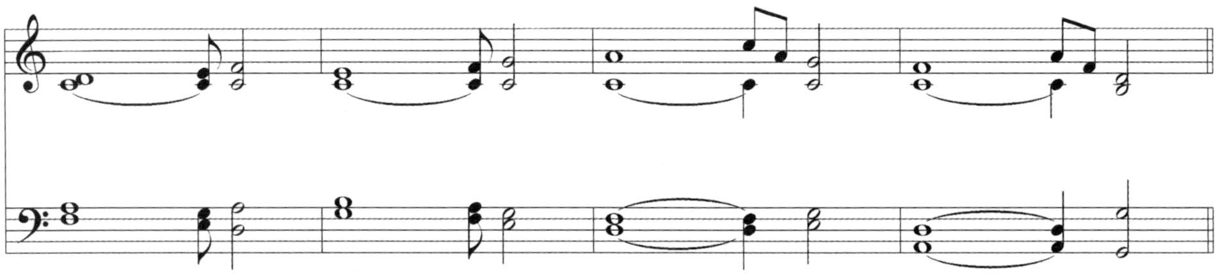

Psalm 84:2-3, 5-6, 9-10. R/ cf. v. 5a

1. How lovely is your dwelling place,
   O LORD of hosts!
   My soul yearns and pines
   for the courts of the LORD.
   [*Repeat mm. 3-4*]
   My heart and my flesh
   cry out for the living God. *R/*

2. Happy they who dwell in your house!
   Continually they praise you.
   Happy the men whose strength you are!
   Their hearts are set upon the pilgrimage. *R/*

3. O LORD of hosts, hear our prayer;
   hearken, O God of Jacob!
   O God, behold our shield,
   and look upon the face of your anointed. *R/*

Anniversary of Dedication of a Church, option 3

Anniversary of Dedication of a Church, option 3, *alternate response*

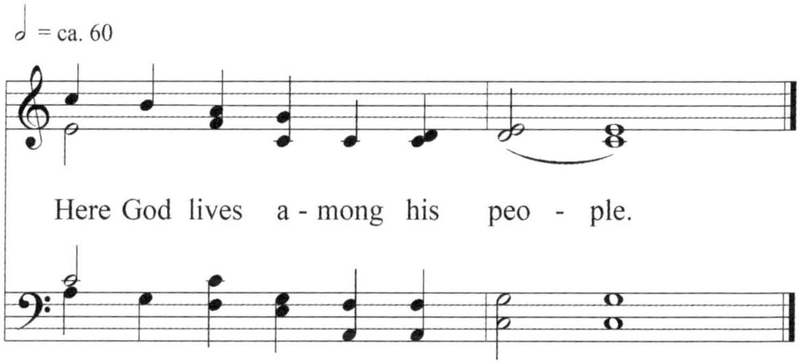

Psalm Tone

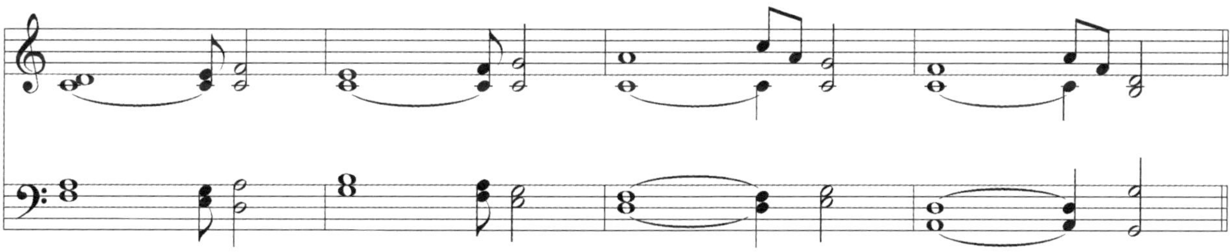

Psalm 84:3, 4, 5, 10, 11. R/ v. 2; Rev 21:3

1. My soul yearns and pines
   for the courts of the Lord.
   My heart and my flesh
   cry out for the living God. *R/*

2. Even the sparrow finds a home,
   and the swallow a nest
   in which she puts her young —
   Your altars, O Lord of hosts,
   my king and my God! *R/*

3. Blessed they who dwell in your house!
   continually they praise you.
   O God, behold our shield,
   and look upon the face of your anointed. *R/*

4. I had rather one day in your courts
   than a thousand elsewhere;
   I had rather lie at the threshold of the house
   of my God
   than dwell in the tents of the wicked. *R/*

Psalm 85

19th Sunday in Ordinary Time, Year A • 2nd Sunday of Advent, Year B • 15th Sunday in Ordinary Time, Year B

Common Advent 2

Psalm Tone

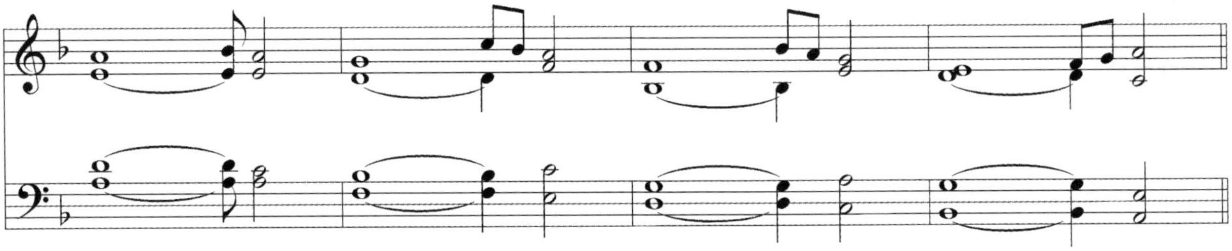

Psalm 85:9-10, 11-12, 13-14. R/ v. 8

1. I will hear what God proclaims;
   the LORD—for he proclaims peace to his people.
   Near indeed is his salvation to those who fear him,
   glory dwelling in our land. *R/*

2. Kindness and truth shall meet;
   justice and peace shall kiss.
   Truth shall spring out of the earth,
   and justice shall look down from heaven. *R/*

3. The LORD himself will give his benefits;
   our land shall yield its increase.
   Justice shall walk before him,
   and prepare the way of his steps. *R/*

Psalm 86

16th Sunday in Ordinary Time, Year A

Psalm Tone

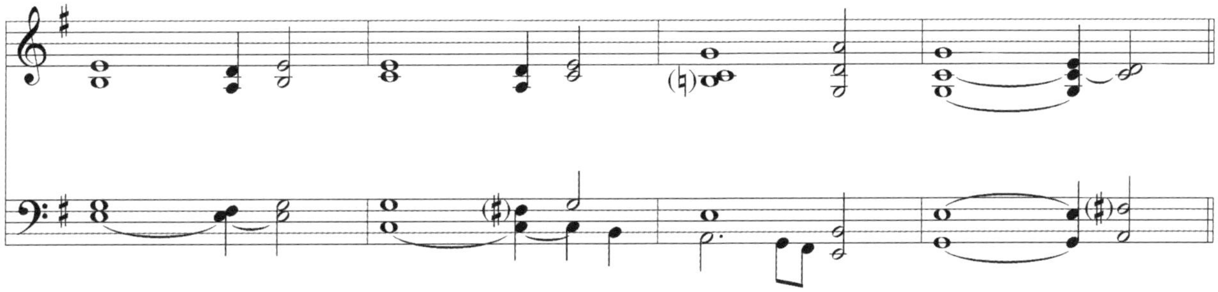

Psalm 86:5-6, 9-10, 15-16. R/ v. 5a

1. You, O LORD, are good and forgiving,
   abounding in kindness to all who call upon you.
   Hearken, O LORD, to my prayer
   and attend to the sound of my pleading. *R/*

2. All the nations you have made shall come
   and worship you, O LORD,
   and glorify your name.
   For you are great, and you do wondrous deeds;
   you alone are God. *R/*

3. You, O LORD, are a God merciful and gracious,
   slow to anger, abounding in kindness and fidelity.
   Turn toward me, and have pity on me;
   give your strength to your servant. *R/*

Psalm 89

4th Sunday of Advent, Year B • Christmas Vigil • 13th Sunday in Ordinary Time, Year A

Psalm Tone

Psalm 89:2-3, 4-5, 16-17, 18-19, 27, 29. R/ v. 2a

4 Advent B
1. - 2. - 3.
Christmas Vigil
2. - 2a. - 3.
13 OT A
1. - 2a. - 3a.

4 Advent B and 13 OT A only [*Christmas Vigil begins at v. 2*]

1. The promises of the LORD I will sing forever;
through all generations my mouth shall proclaim your faithfulness.
For you have said, "My kindness is established forever";
in heaven you have confirmed your faithfulness. *R/*

4 Advent B and Christmas Vigil only

2. "I have made a covenant with my chosen one,
I have sworn to David my servant:
forever will I confirm your posterity
and establish your throne for all generations." *R/*

Christmas Vigil and 13 OT A only

2a. Blessed the people who know the joyful shout;
in the light of your countenance, O LORD, they walk.
At your name they rejoice all the day,
and through your justice they are exalted. *R/*

4 Advent B and Christmas Vigil only

3. "He shall say of me, 'You are my father,
my God, the Rock, my savior.'
Forever I will maintain my kindness toward him,
and my covenant with him stands firm." *R/*

13 OT A only

3a. You are the splendor of their strength,
and by your favor our horn is exalted.
For to the LORD belongs the shield,
and to the Holy One of Israel, our king. *R/*

Psalm 90

28th Sunday in Ordinary Time, Year B

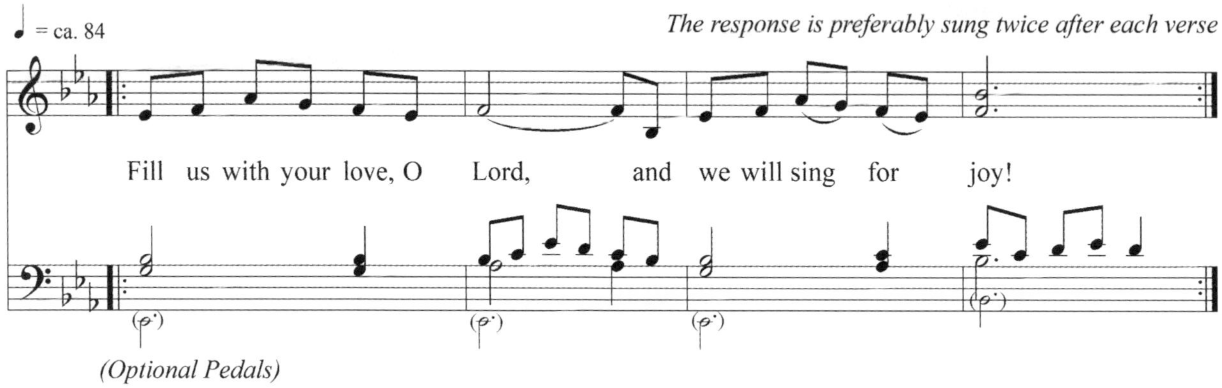

18th Sunday in Ordinary Time, Year C *(Lectionary response)*

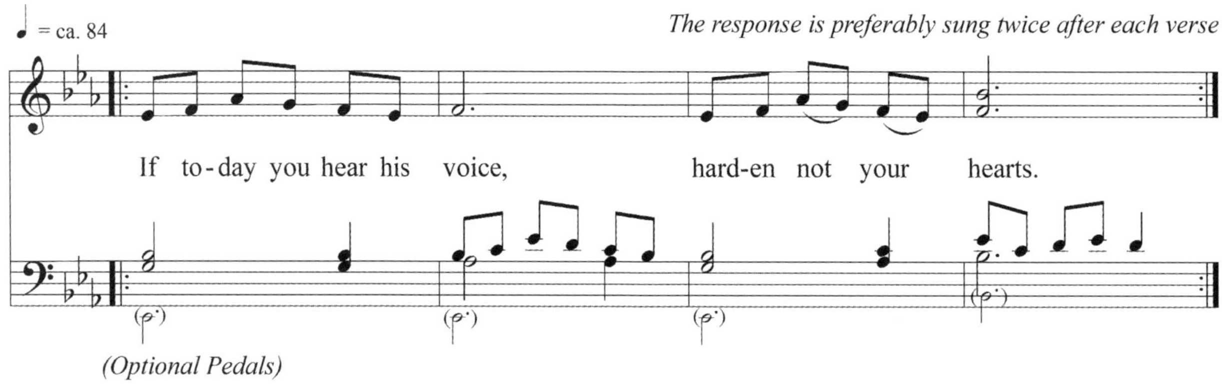

23rd Sunday in Ordinary Time, Year C •
18th Sunday in Ordinary Time, Year C *(correct response)*

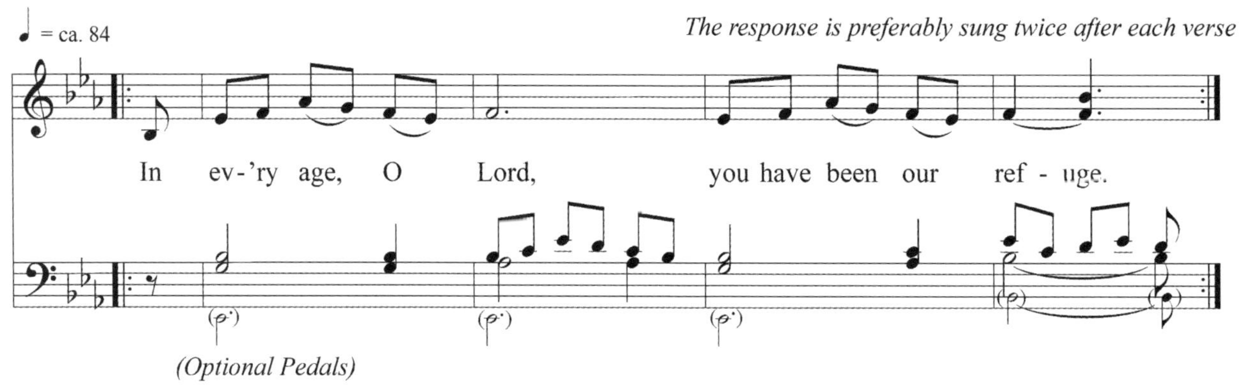

Note:
In the 1969 Lectionary, the **18th Sunday in Ordinary Time, Year C** originally had Psalm 95 with the response *If today you hear his voice....* This was changed in the 1981 Lectionary to Psalm 90, which fits better thematically. However, the compilers of the U.S. 1981 Lectionary overlooked the response, which should also have been changed, and so this day now has Psalm 90 for the verses but still has the original Psalm 95 response *If today you hear his voice...* ! The correct response should have been the same as for the **23rd Sunday in Ordinary Time, Year C**, as indicated above. We provide both responses, enabling communities to choose which they wish to use.

Psalm Tone

28 OT B

Psalm 90:12-13, 14-15, 16-17. R/ v. 14

1. Teach us to number our days aright,
   that we may gain wisdom of heart.
   Return, O LORD! How long?
   Have pity on your servants! *R/*

2. Fill us at daybreak with your kindness,
   that we may shout for joy and gladness all our days.
   Make us glad, for the days when you afflicted us,
   for the years when we saw evil. *R/*

3. Let your work be seen by your servants
   and your glory by their children;
   and may the gracious care of the LORD our God
   be ours;
   prosper the work of our hands for us!
   [*Repeat m. 4*]
   Prosper the work of our hands! *R/*

18 and 23 OT C

Psalm 90:3-4, 5-6, 12-13, 14, 17. R/ v. 1; Ps 95:8

1. You turn man back to dust,
   saying, "Return, O children of men."
   For a thousand years in your sight
   are as yesterday, now that it is past,
   or as a watch of the night. *R/*

2. You make an end of them in their sleep;
   the next morning they are like the changing grass,
   which at dawn springs up anew,
   but by evening wilts and fades. *R/*

3. Teach us to number our days aright,
   that we may gain wisdom of heart.
   Return, O LORD! How long?
   Have pity on your servants! *R/*

4. Fill us at daybreak with your kindness,
   that we may shout for joy and gladness all
   our days.
   And may the gracious care of the LORD our God
   be ours;
   prosper the work of our hands for us!
   [*Repeat m. 4*]
   Prosper the work of our hands! *R/*

Psalm 91

1st Sunday in Lent, Year C • Common Lent 2

Psalm Tone

Psalm 91:1-2, 10-11, 12-13, 14-15. R/ cf. v. 15b

1. You who dwell in the shelter of the Most High,
   who abide in the shadow of the Almighty,
   say to the LORD, "My refuge and fortress,
   my God in whom I trust." *R/*

2. No evil shall befall you,
   nor shall affliction come near your tent,
   for to his angels he has given command about you,
   that they guard you in all your ways. *R/*

3. Upon their hands they shall bear you up,
   lest you dash your foot against a stone.
   You shall tread upon the asp and the viper;
   you shall trample down the lion and the dragon. *R/*

4. Because he clings to me, I will deliver him;
   I will set him on high because he acknowledges my name.
   He shall call upon me, and I will answer him;
   I will be with him in distress; I will deliver him and glorify him. *R/*

Common Lent 2

2a. No evil shall befall you,
   nor affliction come near your tent.
   For God commands the angels
   to guard you in all your ways. *R/*

Psalm 92

11th Sunday in Ordinary Time, Year B • 8th Sunday in Ordinary Time, Year C

Psalm Tone

Psalm 92:2-3, 13-14, 15-16. R/ cf. v. 2a

1. It is good to give thanks to the LORD,
   to sing praise to your name, Most High,
   to proclaim your kindness at dawn
   and your faithfulness throughout the night. *R/*

2. The just one shall flourish like the palm tree,
   like a cedar of Lebanon shall he grow.
   They that are planted in the house of the LORD
   shall flourish in the courts of our God. *R/*

3. They shall bear fruit even in old age;
   vigorous and sturdy shall they be,
   declaring how just is the LORD,
   my rock, in whom there is no wrong. *R/*

Psalm 93

Christ the King, Year B

Psalm Tone

Psalm 93:1, 1-2, 5. R. v/ 1a

1. The LORD is king, in <u>splen</u>dor robed;
   * robed is the LORD and girt a<u>bout</u> with strength. *R/*

2. And he has made the world firm,
   not <u>to</u> be moved.
   Your throne stands firm <u>from</u> of old;
   from everlasting you <u>are</u>, O LORD. *R/*

3. Your decrees are worthy of <u>trust</u> indeed;
   holiness be<u>fits</u> your house,
   O LORD, for <u>length</u> of days. *R/*

Psalm 95

3rd Sunday of Lent, Year A • 23rd Sunday in Ordinary Time, Year A •
4th Sunday in Ordinary Time, Year B • 27th Sunday in Ordinary Time, Year C •
Common Ordinary Time 5

♩ = ca. 84 *The response is preferably sung twice after each verse*

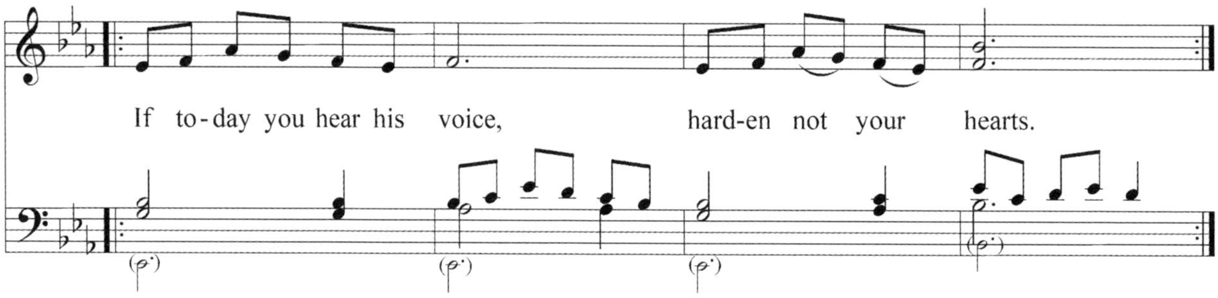

(Optional Pedals)

Psalm Tone

Psalm 95:1-2, 6-7, 8-9. R/ v. 8

1. Come, let us sing joyfully to the LORD;
   let us acclaim the rock of our salvation.
   Let us come into his presence with thanksgiving;
   let us joyfully sing psalms to him. *R/*

2. Come, let us bow down in worship;
   let us kneel before the LORD who made us.
   For he is our God,
   and we are the people he shepherds, the flock he guides. *R/*

3. Oh, that today you would hear his voice:
   "Harden not your hearts as at Meribah,
   as in the day of Massah in the desert,
   where your fathers tempted me;
   they tested me though they had seen my works." *R/*

Note:
In the 1969 Lectionary, this psalm and response were also allocated to the **18th Sunday in Ordinary Time, Year C**. This was changed in the 1981 Lectionary to Psalm 90, which fits better thematically. However, the compilers of the U.S. 1981 Lectionary overlooked the response, which should also have been changed, and so that day now has Psalm 90 for the verses but still has Psalm 95 (*If today you hear his voice....*) for the response!

Anniversary of Dedication of a Church, option 4

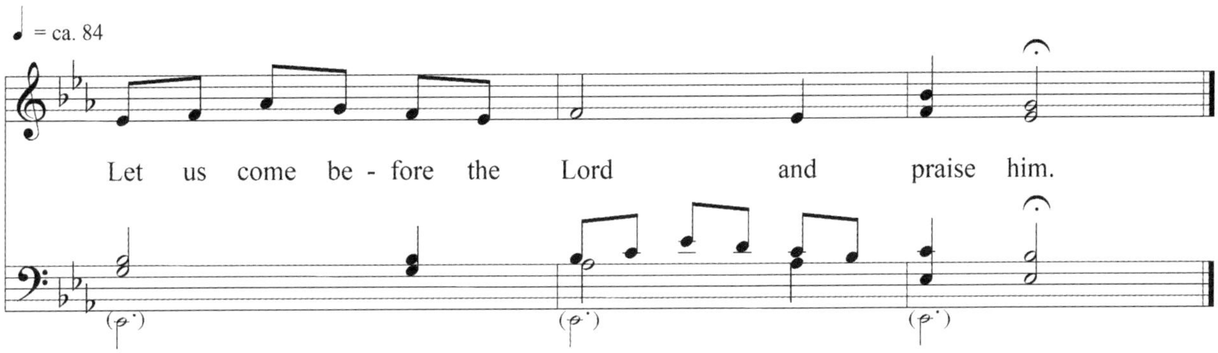

Psalm Tone

Psalm 95:1-2, 3-5, 6-7. R/ v. 2

1. Come, let us sing joyfully to the LORD;
   let us acclaim the Rock of our salvation.
   Let us come into his presence with thanksgiving;
   let us joyfully sing psalms to him. *R/*

2. For the LORD is a great God,
   and a great king above all gods;
   In his hands are the depths of the earth,
   and the tops of the mountains are his.
   [*Repeat mm. 3-4*]
   His is the sea, for he has made it,
   and the dry land, which his hands have formed. *R/*

3. Come, let us bow down in worship;
   let us kneel before the LORD who made us.
   For he is our God,
   and we are the people he shepherds, the flock he guides. *R/*

Psalm 96

Christmas Midnight

29th Sunday in Ordinary Time, Year A

2nd Sunday in Ordinary Time, Year C

Psalm Tone

* *Omit in 3-line verses*

Psalm 96:1-2, 2-3, 4-5, 7-8, 9-10, 11-12, 13. R/ Lk 2:11; v. 7b; v.3

Christmas Midnight and 2 OT C only

1. Sing to the LORD a new song;
   sing to the LORD, all you lands.
   * Sing to the LORD; bless his name. *R/*

Christmas Midnight and 2 OT C only

2. Announce his salvation, day after day.
   Tell his glory among the nations;
   * among all peoples, his wondrous deeds. *R/*

Christmas Midnight only

3. Let the heavens be glad and the earth rejoice;
   let the sea and what fills it resound;
   let the plains be joyful and all that is in them!
   Then shall all the trees of the forest exult. *R/*

Christmas Midnight only

4. They shall exult before the LORD, for he comes;
   for he comes to rule the earth.
   He shall rule the world with justice
   and the peoples with his constancy. *R/*

29 OT A only

1a. Sing to the LORD a new song;
   sing to the LORD, all you lands.
   Tell his glory among the nations;
   among all peoples, his wondrous deeds. *R/*

29 OT A only

2a. For great is the LORD and highly to be praised;
   awesome is he, beyond all gods.
   For all the gods of the nations are things of nought,
   but the LORD made the heavens. *R/*

29 OT A and 2 OT C only

3a. Give to the LORD, you families of nations,
   give to the LORD glory and praise;
   [*] give to the LORD the glory due his name! [*R/*]
   29 OT A only
   Bring gifts and enter his courts. *R/*

29 OT A and 2 OT C only

4a. Worship the LORD in holy attire.
   Tremble before him, all the earth;
   say among the nations: The LORD is king.
   He governs the peoples with equity. *R/*

Christmas Midnight
1. - 2. - 3. - 4.
29 OT A
1a. - 2a. - 3a. - 4a.
2 OT C
1. - 2. - *3a. - 4a.

Psalm 97

Christmas Dawn

Transfiguration (August 6)

Psalm Tone

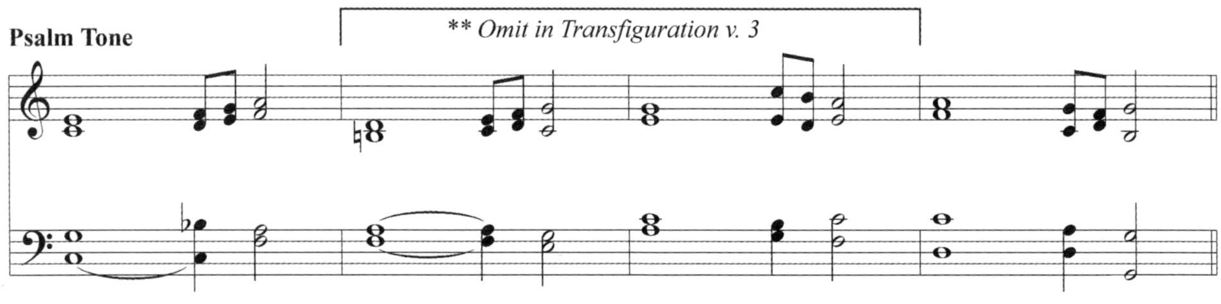

Christmas Dawn
Psalm 97:1, 6, 11-12

1. The LORD is king; let the earth rejoice;
let the many isles be glad.
The heavens proclaim his justice,
and all peoples see his glory. *R/*

2. Light dawns for the just;
and gladness, for the upright of heart.
Be glad in the LORD, you just,
and give thanks to his holy name. *R/*

Transfiguration
Psalm 97:1-2, 5-6, 9. R/ vv. 1 and 9

1. The LORD is king; let the earth rejoice;
let the many islands be glad.
Clouds and darkness are round about him,
justice and judgment are the foundation of his throne. *R/*

2. The mountains melt like wax before the LORD,
before the LORD of all the earth.
The heavens proclaim his justice,
and all peoples see his glory. *R/*

3. Because you, O LORD, are the Most High over all the earth,
** exalted far above all gods. *R/*

7th Sunday of Easter, Year C

7th Sunday of Easter, Year C, *alternate response*

Psalm Tone

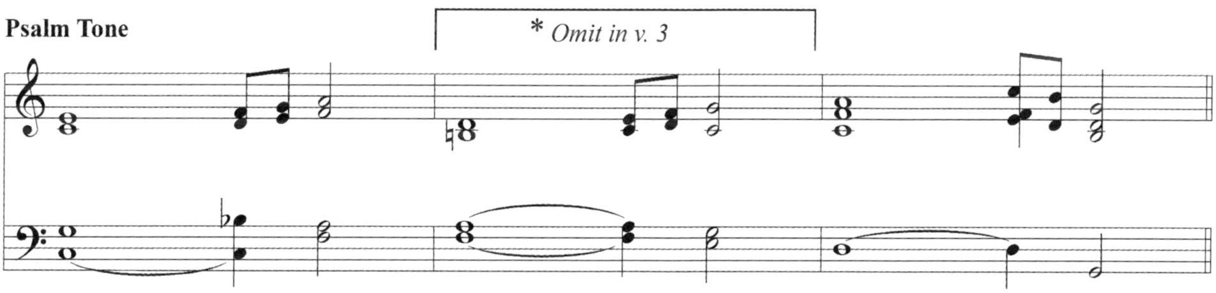

Psalm 97:1-2, 6-7, 9. R/ vv. 1 and 9

1. The Lord is king; let the earth rejoice;
   let the many islands be glad.
   Justice and judgment are the foundation of his throne. *R/*

2. The heavens proclaim his justice,
   and all peoples see his glory.
   All gods are prostrate before him. *R/*

3. You, O Lord, are the Most High over all the earth,
   * exalted far above all gods. *R/*

Psalm 98

Immaculate Conception

Christmas, Mass of the Day • Common Christmas

6th Sunday of Easter, Year B • 28th Sunday in Ordinary Time, Year C

6th Sunday of Easter, Year B, *alternate response*

Psalm Tone

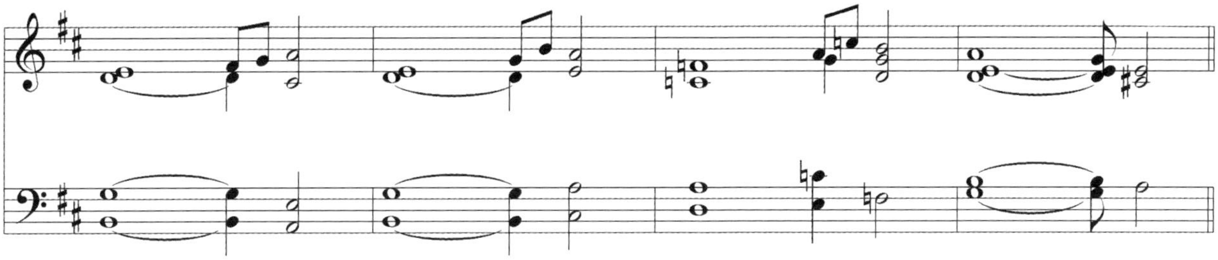

Psalm 98:1, 2-3ab, 3cd-4. R/ v. 1a; 3c; 2b

1. Sing to the LORD a new song,
   for he has done wondrous deeds;
   his right hand has won victory for him,
   his holy arm. *R/*

2. The LORD has made his salvation known:
   in the sight of the nations he has revealed his justice.
   He has remembered his kindness and his faithfulness
   toward the house of Israel. *R/*

3. All the ends of the earth have seen
   the salvation by our God.
   Sing joyfully to the LORD, all you lands;
   break into song; sing praise. *R/*

Christmas Day Mass and Common Christmas only

4. Sing praise to the LORD with the harp,
   with the harp and melodious song.
   With trumpets and the sound of the horn
   sing joyfully before the King, the LORD. *R/*

33rd Sunday in Ordinary Time, Year C

Psalm Tone

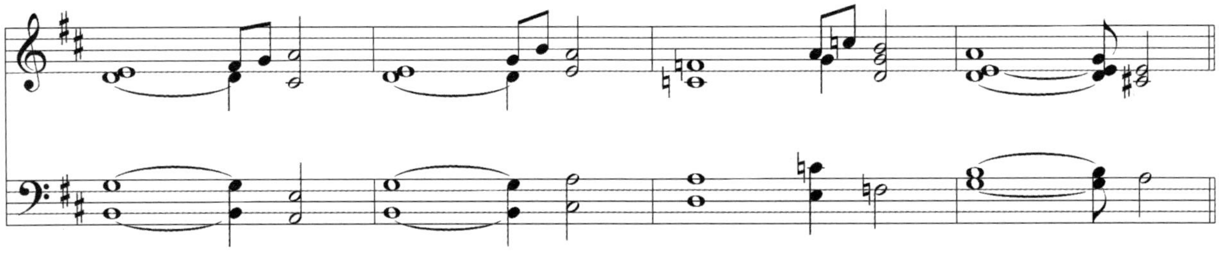

Psalm 98:5-6, 7-8, 9. R/ cf. v. 9

1. Sing praise to the Lord with the harp,
   with the harp and melodious song.
   With trumpets and the sound of the horn
   sing joyfully before the King, the Lord. *R/*

2. Let the sea and what fills it resound,
   the world and those who dwell in it;
   let the rivers clap their hands,
   the mountains shout with them for joy. *R/*

3. Before the Lord, for he comes,
   for he comes to rule the earth;
   he will rule the world with justice
   and the peoples with equity. *R/*

Psalm 100

11th Sunday in Ordinary Time, Year A • 4th Sunday of Easter, Year C • Common Ordinary Time 6

4th Sunday of Easter, Year C, *alternate response*

Psalm Tone

Psalm 100:1-2, 3, 5. R/ v. 3c

1. Sing joyfully to the LORD, all you lands;
   serve the LORD with gladness;
   come before him with joyful song. R/

2. Know that the LORD is God,
   he made us, his we are;
   his people, the flock he tends. R/

3. The LORD is good:
   his kindness endures forever,
   and his faithfulness, to all generations. R/

Psalm 103

7th Sunday in Ordinary Time, Year A • 8th Sunday in Ordinary Time, Year B • 3rd Sunday of Lent, Year C • 7th Sunday in Ordinary Time, Year C • Common Ordinary Time 7

24th Sunday in Ordinary Time, Year A

Psalm Tone

Psalm 103:1-2, 3-4, 6-7, 8, 9, 10, 12-13. R/ v. 8a; v. 8

1. Bless the LORD, O my soul;
 and all my being, bless his holy name.
 Bless the LORD, O my soul,
 and forget not all his benefits. *R/*

2. He pardons all your iniquities,
 heals all your ills.
 He redeems your life from destruction,
 crowns you with kindness and compassion. *R/*

3 Lent C only

3. The LORD secures justice
 and the rights of all the oppressed.
 He has made known his ways to Moses,
 and his deeds to the children of Israel. *R/*

4. Merciful and gracious is the LORD,
 slow to anger, and abounding in kindness.
 Not according to our sins does he deal with us,
 nor does he requite us according to our crimes. *R/*

5. As far as the east is from the west,
 so far has he put our transgressions from us.
 As a father has compassion on his children,
 so the LORD has compassion on those who fear him. *R/*

7 OT A, 8 OT B, 7 OT C, Common OT 7
1. - 2. - 4.- 5.
24 OT A
1. - 2. - 4b. - 5a.
3 Lent C
1. - 2. - 3. - 4a.

3 Lent C only

4a. Merciful and gracious is the LORD,
 slow to anger and abounding in kindness.
 For as the heavens are high above the earth,
 so surpassing is his kindness toward those who fear him. *R/*

24 OT A only

4b. He will not always chide,
 nor does he keep his wrath forever.
 Not according to our sins does he deal with us,
 nor does he requite us according to our crimes. *R/*

24 OT A only

5a. For as the heavens are high above the earth,
 so surpassing is his kindness toward those who fear him.
 As far as the east is from the west,
 so far has he put our transgressions from us. *R/*

7th Sunday of Easter, Year B

♩. = ca. 56

7th Sunday of Easter, Year B, *alternate response*

♩. = ca. 56

Psalm Tone

Psalm 103:1-2, 11-12, 19-20. R. v. 19a

1. Bless the LORD, O my soul;
and all my being, bless his holy name.
Bless the LORD, O my soul,
and forget not all his benefits. *R/*

2. For as the heavens are high above the earth,
so surpassing is his kindness toward those who fear him.
As far as the east is from the west,
so far has he put our transgressions from us. *R/*

3. The LORD has established his throne in heaven,
and his kingdom rules over all.
Bless the LORD, all you his angels,
you mighty in strength, who do his bidding. *R/*

Sacred Heart, Year A

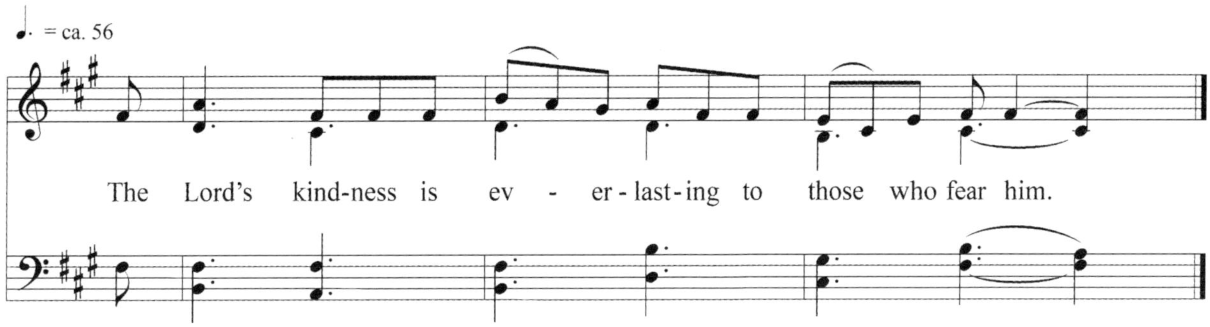

Psalm Tone

Psalm 103:1-2, 3-4, 6-7, 8, 10. R/ cf. v. 17

1. Bless the LORD, O my soul;
   and all my being, bless his holy name.
   Bless the LORD, O my soul,
   and forget not all his benefits. *R/*

2. He pardons all your iniquities,
   heals all your ills.
   He redeems your life from destruction,
   crowns you with kindness and compassion. *R/*

3. Merciful and gracious is the LORD,
   slow to anger, and abounding in kindness.
   Not according to our sins does he deal with us,
   nor does he requite us according to our crimes. *R/*

Psalm 104

Easter Vigil 1 • Pentecost Vigil 4 (and Pentecost Simple Vigil) • Pentecost Day • Common Pentecost

Pentecost Vigil 4 (and Pentecost Simple Vigil), *alternate response* •
Pentecost Day, *alternate response*

Psalm Tone

Easter Vigil 1

Psalm 104:1-2, 5-6, 10, 12, 13-14, 24, 35. R/ cf. v. 30

1. Bless the LORD, O my soul!
   O LORD, my God, you are great indeed!
   You are clothed with majesty and glory,
   robed in light as with a cloak. *R/*

2. You fixed the earth upon its foundation,
   not to be moved forever;
   with the ocean, as with a garment, you covered it;
   above the mountains the waters stood. *R/*

3. You send forth springs into the watercourses
   that wind among the mountains.
   Beside them the birds of heaven dwell;
   from among the branches they send
   forth their song. *R/*

4. You water the mountains from your palace;
   the earth is replete with the fruit of your works.
   You raise grass for the cattle,
   and vegetation for man's use,
   producing bread from the earth. *R/*

5. How manifold are your works, O LORD!
   In wisdom you have wrought them all—
   the earth is full of your creatures.
   Bless the LORD, O my soul! *R/*

Pentecost Vigil 4 (and Pentecost Simple Vigil)

Psalm 104:1-2, 24, 35, 27-28, 29, 30. R/ cf. v. 30

1\. = *v. 1 opposite*

2a. How manifold are your works, O LORD!
In wisdom you have wrought them all—
the earth is full of your creatures.
Bless the LORD, O my soul! Alleluia. *R/*

3a. Creatures all look to you
to give them food in due time.
When you give it to them, they gather it;
when you open your hand, they are filled
with good things. *R/*

4a. If you take away their breath, they perish
and return to their dust.
When you send forth your spirit, they
are created,
and you renew the face of the earth. *R/*

Pentecost Day, Common Pentecost

Psalm 104:1, 24, 29-30, 31, 34. R/ cf. v. 30

1\. = *v. 1 above*

2\. = *v. 4a above*

3. May the glory of the LORD endure forever;
   may the LORD be glad in his works!
   Pleasing to him be my theme;
   I will be glad in the LORD. *R/*

Baptism of the Lord, Year C

Psalm Tone

Psalm 104:1b-2, 3-4, 24-25, 27-28, 29-30. R/ v. 1

1. O Lord, my God, you are great indeed!
   You are clothed with majesty and glory,
   robed in light as with a cloak.
   You have spread out the heavens like a tent-cloth. *R/*

2. You have constructed your palace upon the waters.
   You make the clouds your chariot;
   you travel on the wings of the wind.
   You make the winds your messengers,
   and flaming fire your ministers. *R/*

3. How manifold are your works, O Lord!
   In wisdom you have wrought them all —
   the earth is full of your creatures;
   the sea also, great and wide,
   [*Repeat mm. 3-4*]
   in which are schools without number
   of living things both small and great. *R/*

4. They look to you to give them food in due time.
   When you give it to them, they gather it;
   when you open your hand,
   they are filled with good things. *R/*

5. If you take away their breath,
   they perish and return to the dust.
   When you send forth your spirit, they are created,
   and you renew the face of the earth. *R/*

Psalm 105

Holy Family, Year B

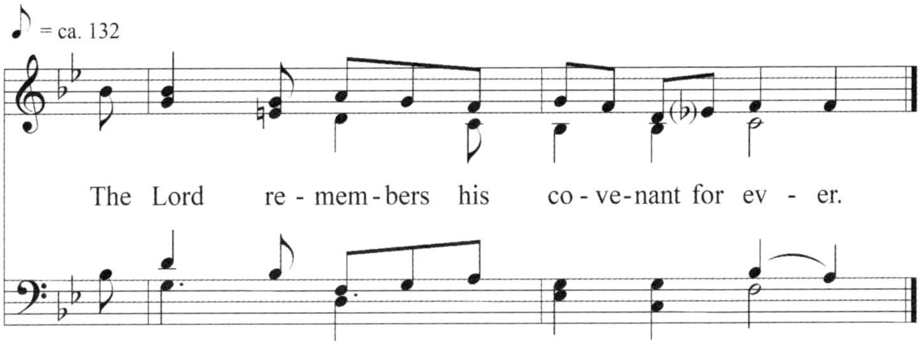

Psalm Tone

Psalm 105:1-2, 3-4, 5-6, 8-9. R/ vv. 7a, 8a

1. Give thanks to the LORD, invoke his name;
   make known among the nations his deeds.
   Sing to him, sing his praise,
   proclaim all his wondrous deeds. *R/*

2. Glory in his holy name;
   rejoice, O hearts that seek the LORD!
   Look to the LORD in his strength;
   constantly seek his face. *R/*

3. You descendants of Abraham, his servants,
   sons of Jacob, his chosen ones!
   He, the LORD, is our God;
   throughout the earth his judgments prevail. *R/*

4. He remembers forever his covenant
   which he made binding for a thousand generations
   which he entered into with Abraham
   and by his oath to Isaac. *R/*

Psalm 107

Pentecost Vigil 3 • 12th Sunday in Ordinary Time, Year B

The response is preferably sung twice each time.

Pentecost Vigil 3, *alternate response* • 12th Sunday in Ordinary Time, *alternate response*

Notes:

The Lectionary Response for 12 OT B has a comma instead of a semicolon after "Lord."

The Alleluia alternate response for 12 OT B is an addition in the 1981 edition of the Lectionary, bringing it into line with the Pentecost Vigil alternate response.

Psalm Tone

Pentecost Vigil 3
Psalm 107:2-3, 4-5, 6-7, 8-9. R/ v. 1b

1. Let the redeemed of the Lord say,
 those whom he has redeemed from the hand of the foe
 And gathered from the lands,
 from the east and the west, from the north and the south. *R/*

2. They went astray in the desert wilderness;
 the way to an inhabited city they did not find.
 Hungry and thirsty,
 their life was wasting away__ within them. *R/*

3. They cried to the Lord in their distress;
 from their straits__ he rescued them.
 And he led them by a direct way
 to reach an inhabited city. *R/*

4. Let them give thanks to the Lord for his mercy
 and his wondrous deeds to the children of men,
 Because he satisfied the longing soul
 and filled the hungry soul with good things. *R/*

12 OT B
Psalm 107:23-24, 25-26, 28-29, 30-31. R/ v. 1b

1. They who sailed the sea in ships,
 trading on the deep waters,
 these saw the works of the Lord
 and his wonders in the abyss. *R/*

2. His command raised up a storm wind
 which tossed its waves__ on high.
 They mounted up to heaven; they sank to the depths;
 their hearts melted away in their plight. *R/*

3. They cried to the Lord in their distress;
 from their straits__ he rescued them,
 he hushed the storm to a gentle breeze,
 and the billows of the sea__ were stilled. *R/*

4. They rejoiced that they were calmed,
 and he brought them to their desired haven.
 Let them give thanks to the Lord for his kindness
 and his wondrous deeds to the children of men. *R/*

Note:
Verse 1 for the Pentecost Vigil erroneously has an uppercase A at the beginning of line 3, even though the sentence continues.

Psalm 110

Corpus Christi, Year C

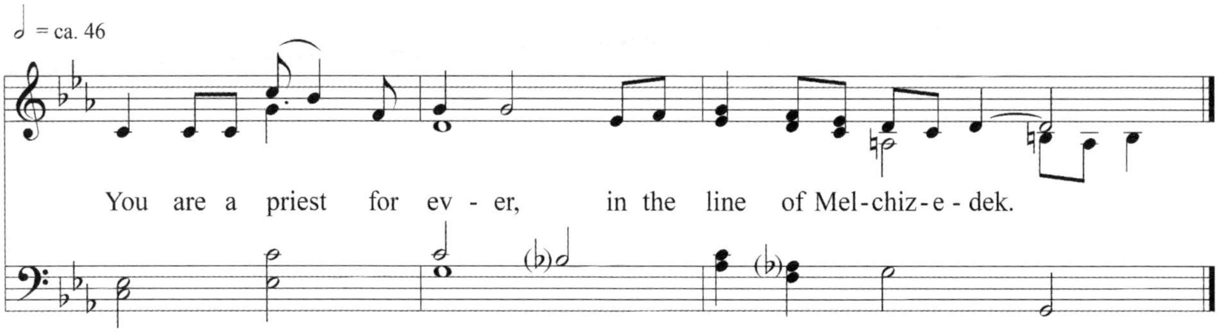

Psalm Tone

Psalm 110:1, 2, 3, 4. R/ v. 4b

1. The LORD said to my Lord:
   "Sit at my right hand
   till I make your enemies your footstool." *R/*

2. The scepter of your power
   the LORD will stretch forth from Zion:
   "Rule in the midst of your enemies." *R/*

3. "Yours is princely power in the day of your birth,
   in holy splendor;
   before the daystar, like the dew, I have begotten you." *R/*

4. The LORD has sworn, and he will not repent:
   "You are a priest forever,
   according to the order of Melchizedek." *R/*

Psalm 112

5th Sunday in Ordinary Time, Year A

5th Sunday in Ordinary Time, Year A, *alternate response*

Note:
The alternate response is an addition in the 1981 Lectionary.

Psalm Tone

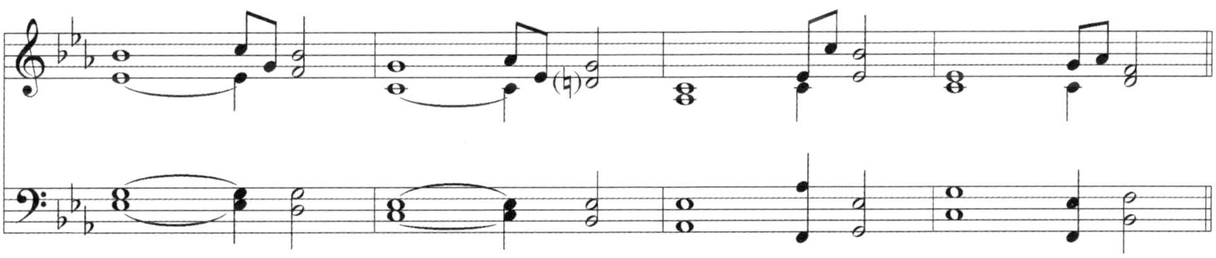

Psalm 112:4-5, 6-7, 8-9. R/ v. 4a

1. Light shines through the darkness for the upright;
   he is gracious and merciful and just.
   Well for the man who is gracious and lends,
   who conducts his affairs with justice. *R/*

2. He shall never be moved;
   the just one shall be in everlasting remembrance.
   An evil report he shall not fear;
   his heart is firm, trusting in the Lord. *R/*

3. His heart is steadfast; he shall not fear.
   Lavishly he gives to the poor;
   his justice shall endure forever;
   his horn shall be exalted in glory. *R/*

Psalm 113

25th Sunday in Ordinary Time, Year C

Note:
Some Lectionaries have no comma after 'Lord' in the response.

25th Sunday in Ordinary Time, Year C, *alternate response*

Psalm Tone

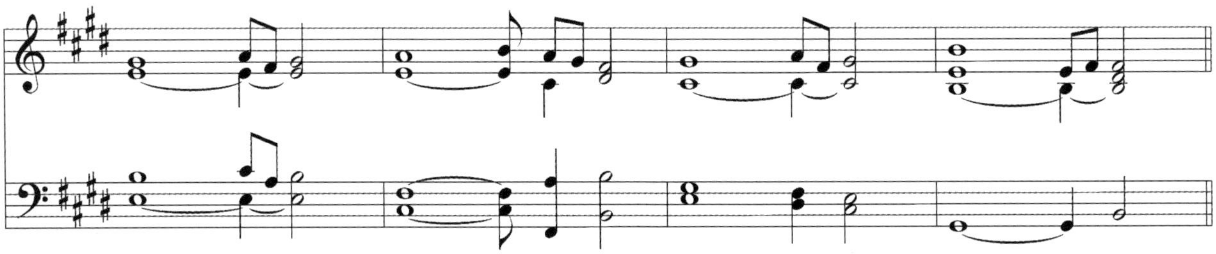

Psalm 113:1-2, 4-6, 7-8. R/ vv. 1a, 7b

1. Praise, you servants of the Lord,
   praise the name of the Lord.
   Blessed be the name of the Lord
   both now and forever. *R/*

2. High above all nations is the Lord;
   above the heavens is his glory.
   Who is like the Lord, our God, who is enthroned on high
   and looks upon the heavens and the earth below? *R/*

3. He raises up the lowly from the dust;
   from the dunghill he lifts up the poor
   to seat them with princes,
   with the princes of his own people. *R/*

Psalm 116

2nd Sunday of Lent, Year B • 24th Sunday in Ordinary Time, Year B

24th Sunday in Ordinary Time, Year B, *alternate response*

Psalm Tone

24 OT B
Psalm 116:1-2, 3-4, 5-6, 8-9. R/ v. 9

1. I love the LORD because he has heard
   my voice in supplication,
   because he has inclined his ear to me
   the day I called. *R/*

2. The cords of death encompassed me;
   the snares of the netherworld seized upon me;
   I fell into distress and sorrow,
   and I called upon the name of the LORD,
      "O LORD, save my life!" *R/*

3. Gracious is the LORD and just;
   yes, our God is merciful.
   The LORD keeps the little ones;
   I was brought low, and he saved me. *R/*

4. For he has freed my soul from death,
   my eyes from tears, my feet from stumbling.
   I shall walk before the LORD
   in the land of the living. *R/*

2 Lent B
Psalm 116:10, 15, 16-17, 18-19. R/ v. 9

1. I believed, even when I said,
   "I am greatly afflicted."
   Precious in the eyes of the LORD
   is the death of his faithful ones. *R/*

2. O LORD, I am your servant;
   I am your servant, the son of your handmaid;
   you have loosed my bonds.
   To you will I offer sacrifice of thanksgiving,
      and I will call upon the name of the LORD. *R/*

3. My vows to the LORD I will pay
   in the presence of all his people,
   In the courts of the house of the LORD,
   in your midst, O Jerusalem. *R/*

Holy Thursday, Evening Mass of the Lord's Supper

Body and Blood of Christ, Year B

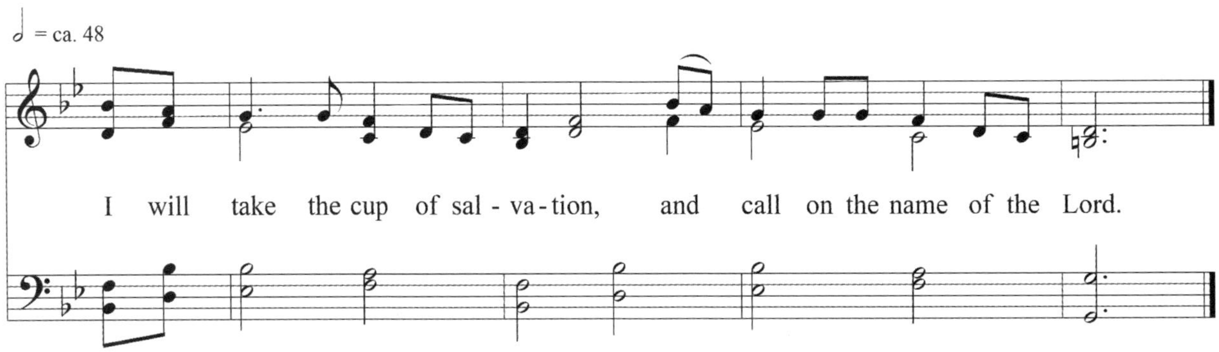

Body and Blood of Christ, Year B, *alternate response*

Psalm Tone

Psalm 116:12-13, 15-16bc, 17-18. R/ cf. 1 Cor 10:16; v. 13

1. How shall I make a return to the LORD
   for all the good he has done for me?
   The cup of salvation I will take up,
   and I will call upon the name of the LORD. *R/*

2. Precious in the eyes of the LORD
   is the death of his faithful ones.
   I am your servant, the son of your handmaid;
   you have loosed my bonds. *R/*

3. To you will I offer sacrifice of thanksgiving,
   and I will call upon the name of the LORD.
   My vows to the LORD I will pay
   in the presence of all his people. *R/*

Psalm 117

9th Sunday in Ordinary Time, Year C • 21st Sunday in Ordinary Time, Year C

Alternate response (both Sundays)

Psalm Verses *Psalm 117:1, 2. R/ Mk 16:15*

* *If the quadruplet is too difficult, use* [rhythm] *instead.*

Note:
Some Lectionaries have lowercase 'good news' in 9 OT C response.

Psalm 118

Easter Vigil Alleluia Psalm • Easter Day, *alternate response*

Second harmonization for initial repeat. After subsequent verses, select either harmonization.

Easter Day • Easter Common 1

Psalm Tone

Psalm 118:1-2, 16-17, 22-23. R/ v. 24

1. Give thanks to the LORD, for he is good,
   for his mercy endures forever.
   Let the house of Israel say,
   "His mercy endures forever." *R/*

2. The right hand of the LORD has struck with power;
   the right hand of the LORD is exalted.
   I shall not die, but live,
   and declare the works of the LORD. *R/*

3. The stone the builders rejected
   has become the cornerstone.
   By the LORD has this been done;
   it is wonderful in our eyes. *R/*

Note:
Lectionary for **Easter Sunday** has the whole of v. 2 in quotation marks.
Lectionary for **Easter Common Psalm 1** reverses the first two lines of v. 2.

2nd Sunday of Easter, Years A-B-C

4th Sunday of Easter, Year B

2nd Sunday of Easter, Years A-B-C, *alternate response* •
4th Sunday of Easter, Year B, *alternate response*

Second harmonization for initial repeat. After subsequent verses, select either harmonization.

Psalm Tone

2 Easter A-B-C
Psalm 118:2-4, 13-15, 22-24. R/ v. 1

1. Let the house of Israel say,
"His mercy endures forever."
Let the house of Aaron say,
"His mercy endures forever."
Let those who fear the LORD say,
"His mercy endures forever." *R/*

2. I was hard pressed and was falling,
but the LORD helped me.
My strength and my courage is the LORD,
and he has been my savior.
The joyful shout of victory
in the tents of the just: *R/*

3. The stone which the builders rejected
has become the cornerstone.
By the LORD has this been done;
it is wonderful in our eyes.
This is the day the LORD has made;
let us be glad and rejoice in it. *R/*

4 Easter B
Psalm 118:1, 8-9, 21-23, 26, 28, 29. R/ v. 22

1. Give thanks to the LORD, for he is good,
for his mercy endures forever.
It is better to take refuge in the LORD
than to trust in man.
It is better to take refuge in the LORD
than to trust in princes. *R/*

2. I will give thanks to you, for you have answered me
and have been my savior.
The stone which the builders rejected
has become the cornerstone.
By the LORD has this been done;
it is wonderful in our eyes. *R/*

3. Blessed is he who comes in the name of the LORD;
we bless you from the house of the LORD.
I will give thanks to you, for you have answered me
and have been my savior.
Give thanks to the LORD, for he is good;
for his kindness endures forever. *R/*

Psalm 119

6th Sunday in Ordinary Time, Year A

17th Sunday in Ordinary Time, Year A

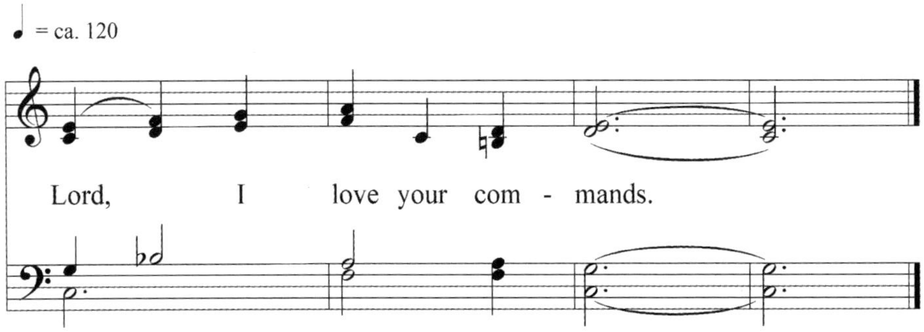

Psalm Tone

6 OT A

Psalm 119:1-2, 4-5, 17-18, 33-34. R/ v. 1b

1. Blessed are they whose way is blameless,
   who walk in the law of the LORD.
   Blessed are they who observe his decrees,
   who seek him with all their heart. *R/*

2. You have commanded that your precepts
   be diligently kept.
   Oh, that I might be firm in the ways
   of keeping your statutes! *R/*

3. Be good to your servant, that I may live
   and keep your words.
   Open my eyes, that I may consider
   the wonders of your law. *R/*

4. Instruct me, O LORD, in the way of your statutes,
   that I may exactly observe them.
   Give me discernment, that I may observe your law
   and keep it with all my heart. *R/*

17 OT A

Psalm 119:57, 72, 76-77, 127-128, 129-130. R/ v. 97a

1. I have said, O LORD, that my part
   is to keep your words.
   The law of your mouth is to me more precious
   than thousands of gold and silver pieces. *R/*

2. Let your kindness comfort me
   according to your promise to your servants.
   Let your compassion come to me that I may live,
   for your law is my delight. *R/*

3. For I love your command
   more than gold, however fine.
   For in all your precepts I go forward;
   every false way I hate. *R/*

4. Wonderful are your decrees;
   therefore I observe them.
   The revelation of your words sheds light,
   giving understanding to the simple. *R/*

Psalm 121

29th Sunday in Ordinary Time, Year C

Psalm Tone

Psalm 121:1-2, 3-4, 5-6, 7-8. R/ cf. v. 2

1. I lift up my eyes toward the mountains;
   whence shall help come to me?
   My help *is* from the Lord,
   who made heaven and earth. *R/*

2. May he not suffer your foot to slip;
   may he slumber not who guards you:
   indeed he neither slumbers nor sleeps,
   the guardian of Israel. *R/*

3. The Lord is your guardian; the Lord is your shade;
   he is beside you at your right hand.
   The sun shall not harm you by day,
   nor the moon by night. *R/*

4. The Lord will guard you from all evil;
   he will guard your life.
   The Lord will guard your com*ing* and your going,
   both now and forever. *R/*

Psalm 122

1st Sunday of Advent, Year A • Christ the King, Year C •
Common Ordinary Time 9 (last weeks) • Anniversary of Dedication of a Church, option 5

Psalm Tone

Psalm 122:1-2, 3-4, 4-5, 6-7, 8-9. R/ cf. v. 1

1. I rejoiced because they said to me,
   "We will go up to the house of the Lord."
   And now we have set foot
   within your gates, O Jerusalem. *R/*

2. Jerusalem, built as a city
   with compact unity.
   To it the tribes go up,
   the tribes of the Lord. *R/*

Omit on Anniversary of Dedication

3. According to the decree for Israel,
   to give thanks to the name of the Lord.
   In it are set up judgment seats,
   seats for the house of David. *R/*

Note:
Anniversary of Dedication 5, v. 5, line 1, has
"Because of my relatives and friends"

1 Advent A, Common OT 9
1. - 2. - 3. - 4. - 5.
Christ the King C
1. - 2. - 3.
Anniversary of Dedication 5
1. - 2. - 5.

Omit on Christ the King C and Anniversary of Dedication

4. Pray for the peace of Jerusalem!
   May those who love you prosper!
   May peace be within your walls,
   prosperity in your buildings. *R/*

5. Because of my brothers and friends
   I will say, "Peace be within you!"
   Because of the house of the Lord, our God,
   I will pray for your good. *R/*

Psalm 123

14th Sunday in Ordinary Time, Year B

Psalm Tone

Psalm 123:1-2, 2, 3-4. R/ v. 2cd

1. To you I lift up my eyes
   who are enthroned in heaven —
   as the eyes of servants
   are on the hands of their masters. *R/*

2. As the eyes of a maid
   are on the hands of her mistress,
   so are our eyes on the LORD, our God,
   till he have pity on us. *R/*

3. Have pity on us, O LORD, have pity on us,
   for we are more than sated with contempt;
   our souls are more than sated
   with the mockery of the arrogant,
   with the contempt of the proud. *R/*

Psalm 126

30th Sunday in Ordinary Time, Year B • 2nd Sunday of Advent, Year C •
5th Sunday of Lent, Year C

Psalm Tone

Psalm 126:1-2, 2-3, 4-5, 6. R/ v. 3

1. When the LORD brought back the captives of Zion,
   we were like men dreaming.
   Then our mouth was filled with laughter,
   and our tongue with rejoicing. *R/*

2. Then they said among the nations,
   "The LORD has done great things for them."
   The LORD has done great things for us;
   we are glad indeed. *R/*

3. Restore our fortunes, O LORD,
   like the torrents in the southern desert.
   Those who sow in tears
   shall reap rejoicing. *R/*

4. Although they go forth weeping,
   carrying the seed to be sown,
   they shall come back rejoicing,
   carrying their sheaves. *R/*

Psalm 128

Holy Family

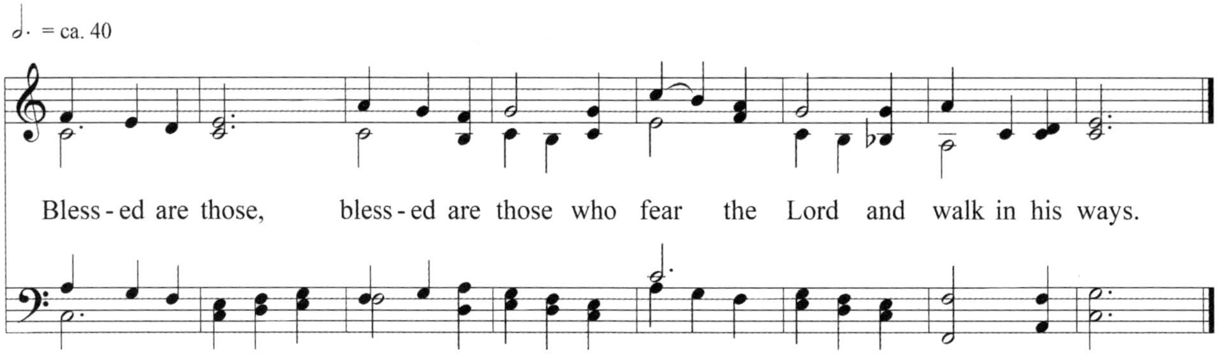

27th Sunday in Ordinary Time, Year B

33rd Sunday in Ordinary Time, Year A

Psalm Tone

Psalm 128:1-2, 3, 4-5, 6 R/ cf. v. 1; cf. v. 5; cf. v. 1a

Holy Family only

1. Blessed is everyone who fears the LORD,
 who walks in his ways!
 For you shall eat the fruit of your handiwork;
 blessed shall you be, and favored. *R/*

27 OT B and 33 OT A only

1a. Blessed are you who fear the LORD,
 who walk in his ways!
 For you shall eat the fruit of your handiwork;
 blessed shall you be, and favored. *R/*

2. Your wife shall be like a fruitful vine
 in the recesses of your home;
 your children like olive plants
 around your table. *R/*

3. Behold, thus is the man blessed
 who fears the LORD.
 The LORD bless you from Zion:
 may you see the prosperity of Jerusalem
 all the days of your life. *R/*

27 OT B only

4. ** May you see your children's children.
 Peace be upon Israel! *R/*

Holy Family
1. - 2. - 3.
27 OT B
1a. - 2. - 3. - 4.
33 OT A
1a. - 2. - 3.

Psalm 130

5th Sunday of Lent, Year A • 10th Sunday in Ordinary Time, Year B • Common Lent 3

Psalm Tone

5 Lent A, 10 OT B
Psalm 130:1-2, 3-4, 5-6, 7-8. R/ v. 7bc

1. Out of the depths I cry to you, O LORD;
   LORD, hear my voice!
   Let your ears be attentive
   to my voice in supplication. *R/*

2. If you, O LORD, mark iniquities,
   LORD, who can stand?
   But with you is forgiveness,
   that you may be revered. *R/*

3. I trust in the LORD;
   my soul trusts in his word.
   More than sentinels wait for the dawn,
   let Israel wait for the LORD. *R/*

4. For with the LORD is kindness
   and with him is plenteous redemption;
   and he will redeem Israel
   from all their iniquities. *R/*

Common Lent 3
Psalm 130:1-2, 3-4, 4-6, 7-8. R/ v. 7bc

1. Out of the depths I cry to you, O LORD;
   LORD, hear my voice!
   Let your ears be attentive
   to my voice in supplication. *R/*

2. If you, O LORD, mark iniquities,
   LORD, who can stand?
   But with you is forgiveness,
   and so you may be revered. *R/*

3. I trust in the LORD;
   my soul trusts in his word.
   My soul waits for the LORD
   more than sentinels wait for the dawn. *R/*

4. For with the LORD is kindness
   and with him is plenteous redemption;
   and he will redeem Israel
   from all their iniquities. *R/*

Psalm 131

31st Sunday in Ordinary Time, Year A

Psalm Tone

Psalm 131:1, 2, 3

1. O Lord, my heart is not proud,
   nor are my eyes haughty;
   I busy not myself with great things,
   nor with things too sublime for me. *R/*

2. Nay rather, I have stilled and quieted
   my soul like a weaned child.
   Like a weaned child on its mother's lap,
   so is my soul within me. *R/*

3. **
   O Israel, hope in the Lord,
   both now and forever. *R/*

Psalm 132

Assumption, Vigil

Psalm Tone

Psalm 132:6-7, 9-10, 13-14. R/ v. 8

1. Behold, we heard of it in Ephrathah;
   we found it in the fields of Jaar.
   Let us enter his dwelling,
   let us worship at his footstool. *R/*

2. May your priests be clothed with justice;
   let your faithful ones shout merrily for joy.
   For the sake of David your servant,
   reject not the plea of your anointed. *R/*

3. For the LORD has chosen Zion;
   he prefers her for his dwelling.
   "Zion is my resting place forever;
   in her will I dwell, for I prefer her." *R/*

Psalm 136

Common Easter Vigil 1 and 2

Common Easter Vigil 1
Psalm 136:1-3, 4-6, 7-9, 24-26.

1. Give thanks to the LORD, for he is good,
   for his mercy endures forever;
   give thanks to the God of gods,
   for his mercy endures forever;
   give thanks to the LORD of lords,
   for his mercy endures forever. *R/*

2. Who alone does great wonders,
   for his mercy endures forever;
   who made the heavens in wisdom,
   for his mercy endures forever;
   who spread out the earth upon the waters,
   for his mercy endures forever. *R/*

3. Who made the great lights,
   for his mercy endures forever;
   the sun to rule over the day,
   for his mercy endures forever;
   the moon and the stars to rule over the night,
   for his mercy endures forever. *R/*

4. Who freed us from our foes,
   for his mercy endures forever;
   who gives food to all flesh,
   for his mercy endures forever;
   give thanks to the God of heaven,
   for his mercy endures forever. *R/*

Common Easter Vigil 2
Psalm 136:1, 3, 16, 21-23, 24-26.

1. Give thanks to the LORD, for he is good,
   for his mercy endures forever;
   give thanks to the LORD of lords,
   for his mercy endures forever;
   who led his people through the wilderness,
   for his mercy endures forever. *R/*

2. Who made their land a heritage,
   for his mercy endures forever;
   the heritage of Israel, his servant,
   for his mercy endures forever;
   who remembered us in our abjection,
   for his mercy endures forever. *R/*

3. Who freed us from our foes,
   for his mercy endures forever;
   who gives food to all flesh,
   for his mercy endures forever;
   give thanks to the God of heaven,
   for his mercy endures forever. *R/*

Psalm 137

4th Sunday of Lent, Year B

Psalm Tone

Psalm 137:1-2, 3, 4-5, 6. R/ v. 6ab

1. By the streams of Babylon
   we sat and wept
   when we remembered Zion.
   On the aspens of that land
   we hung up our harps. *R/*

2. For there our captors asked of us
   the lyrics of our songs,
   and our despoilers urged us to be joyous:
   "Sing for us the songs of Zion!" *R/*

3. How could we sing a song of the LORD
   in a foreign land?
   If I forget you, Jerusalem,
   may my right hand be forgotten! *R/*

4. May my tongue cleave to my palate
   if I remember you not,
   if I place not Jerusalem
   ahead of my joy. *R/*

Psalm 138

21st Sunday in Ordinary Time, Year A

5th Sunday in Ordinary Time, Year C

17th Sunday in Ordinary Time, Year C

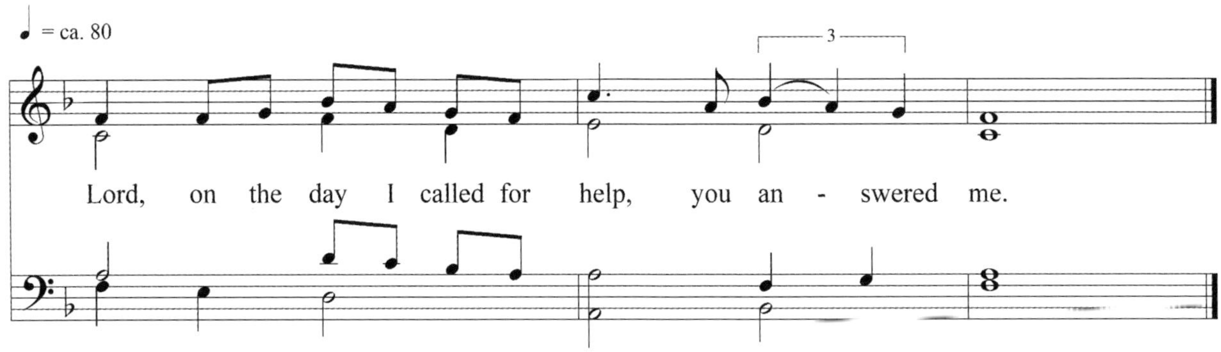

Thanksgiving, option 3

Psalm Tone

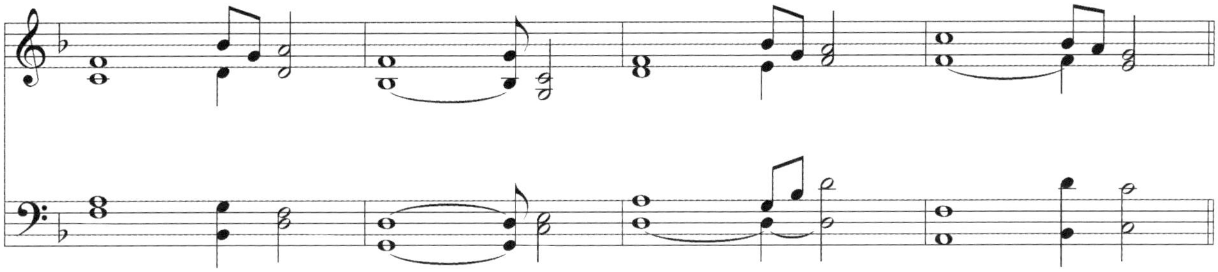

Thanksgiving 3
Psalm 138:1-2ab, 2cde-3, 4-5. R/ v. 2bc

1. I will give thanks to you, O LORD,
 with all my heart,
 for you have heard the words of my mouth;
 in the presence of the angels I will
 sing your praise;
 I will worship at your holy temple. *R/*

2. I will give thanks to your name,
 because of your kindness and your truth.
 When I called, you answered me;
 you built up strength within me. *R/*

3. All the kings of the earth shall give thanks to
 you, O LORD,
 when they hear the words of your mouth;
 And they shall sing of the ways of the LORD:
 "Great is the glory of the LORD." *R/*

21 OT A
Psalm 138:1-2, 2-3, 6, 8. R/ v. 8bc

1., 2. *as above*

3b. The LORD is exalted, yet the lowly he sees,
 and the proud he knows from afar.
 Your kindness, O LORD, endures forever;
 forsake not the work of your hands. *R/*

5 OT C
Psalm 138:1-2, 2-3, 4-5, 7-8. R/ v. 1c

1a. I will give thanks to you, O LORD, with all my heart,
 for you have heard the words of my mouth;
 in the presence of the angels I will sing your praise;
 I will worship at your holy temple and give
 thanks to your name. *R/*

2a. Because of your kindness and your truth;
 for you have made great above all things
 your name and your promise.
 When I called, you answered me;
 you built up strength within me. *R/*

3. *as opposite*

4. Your right hand saves me.
 The LORD will complete what he has done
 for me;
 your kindness, O LORD, endures forever;
 forsake not the work of your hands. *R/*

17 OT C
Psalm 138:1-2, 2-3, 6-7, 7-8. R/ v. 3a

1a., 2a. *as above*

3a. The LORD is exalted, yet the lowly he sees,
 and the proud he knows from afar.
 Though I walk amid distress, you preserve me;
 against the anger of my enemies you
 raise your hand. *R/*

4. = *4 above*

Thanksgiving 1. - 2. - 3.	**5 OT C** 1a. - 2a. - 3. - 4.
21 OT A 1. - 2. - 3b.	**17 OT C** 1a. - 2a. - 3a. - 4.

Psalm 139

St. John the Baptist, Day Mass

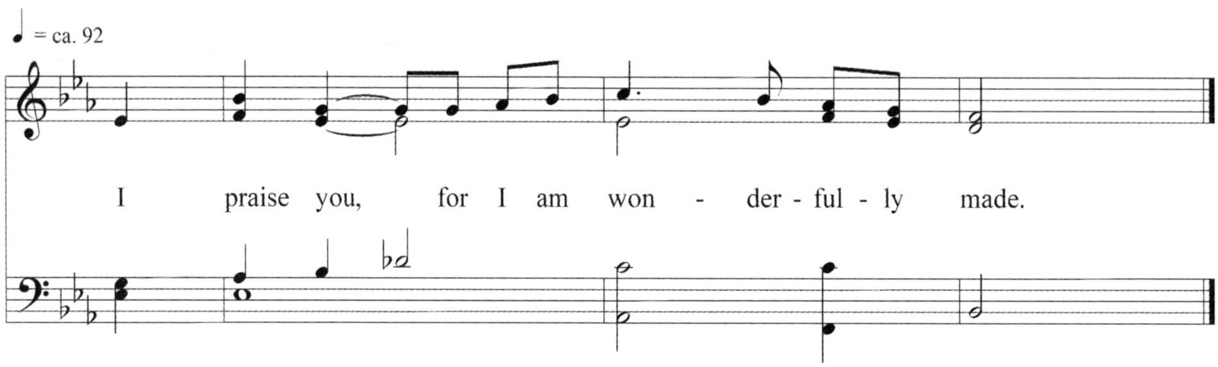

Psalm Tone

Psalm 139:1b-3, 13-14ab, 14c-15. R/ v. 14

1. O Lord, you have probed me, you know me:
   you know when I sit and when I stand;
   § you understand my thoughts from afar.
   My journeys and my rest you scrutinize,
   with all my ways you are familiar. *R/*

2. Truly you have formed my inmost being;
   you knit me in my mother's womb.
   I give you thanks that I am fearfully, wonderfully made;
   wonderful are your works. *R/*

3. My soul also you knew full well;
   nor was my frame unknown to you
   When I was made in secret,
   when I was fashioned in the depths of the earth. *R/*

Psalm 145

14th Sunday in Ordinary Time, Year A • 5th Sunday of Easter, Year C •
31st Sunday in Ordinary Time, Year C • Common Ordinary Time 8

Thanksgiving, option 4

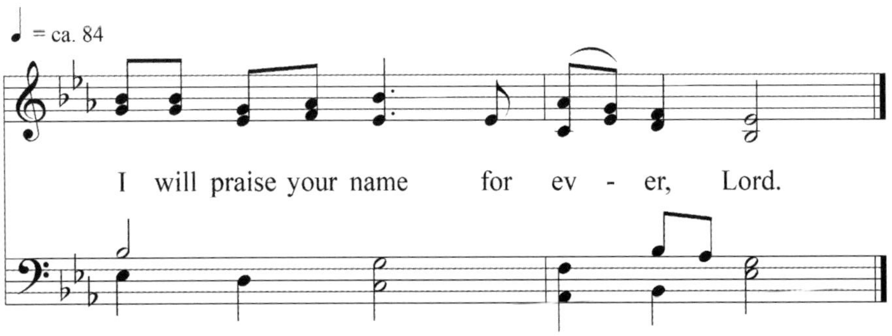

14th Sunday in Ordinary Time, *alternate response* •
5th Sunday of Easter, Year C, *alternate response*

Psalm Tone

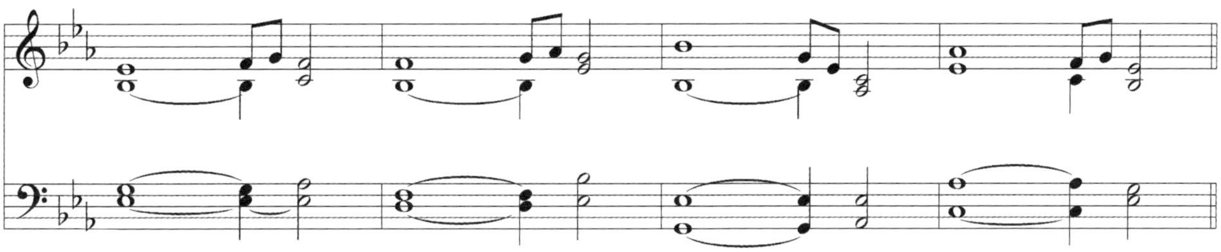

14 OT A, 31 OT C, Common OT 8
Psalm 145:1-2, 8-9, 10-11, 13-14. R. cf. v. 1

1. I will extol you, O my God and King,
and I will bless your name forever and ever.
Every day will I bless you,
and I will praise your name forever and ever. *R/*

2. The LORD is gracious and merciful,
slow to anger and of great kindness.
The LORD is good to all
and compassionate toward all his works. *R/*

3. Let all your works give you thanks, O LORD,
and let your faithful ones bless you.
Let them discourse of the glory of your kingdom
and speak of your might. *R/*

4. The LORD is faithful in all his words
and holy in all his works.
The LORD lifts up all who are falling
and raises up all who are bowed down. *R/*

Thanksgiving 4
Psalm 145:2-3, 4-5, 6-7, 8-9, 10-11. R/ cf. v. 1

1a. Every day will I bless you,
and I will praise your name forever and ever.
Great is the LORD and highly to be praised;
his greatness is unsearchable. *R/*

2a. Generation after generation praises your works
and proclaims your might.
They speak of the splendor of your glorious majesty
and tell of your wondrous works. *R/*

3a. They discourse of the power of your terrible deeds
and declare your greatness.
They publish the fame of your abundant goodness
and joyfully sing of your justice. *R/*

4a. = *2. opposite*

5a. = *3. opposite*

5 Easter C
Psalm 145:8-9, 10-11, 12-13. R/ cf. v. 1

1b. = *2. above*

2b. = *3. above*

3b. Let them make known your might to the children of Adam,
and the glorious splendor of your kingdom.
Your kingdom is a kingdom for all ages,
and your dominion endures through all generations. *R/*

14 OT A, 31 OT C, Common OT 8
1. - 2. - 3. - 4.
5 Easter C
2. - 3. - 3b.
Thanksgiving 4
1a. - 2a. - 3a. - 2. - 3.

18th Sunday in Ordinary Time, Year A • 17th Sunday in Ordinary Time, Year B

Psalm Tone

Psalm 145:8-9, 10-11, 15-16, 17-18. R/ cf. v. 16

18 OT A only

1. The LORD is gracious and merciful,
   slow to anger and of great kindness.
   The LORD is good to all
   and compassionate toward all his works. *R/*

2. The eyes of all look hopefully to you,
   and you give them their food in due season;
   you open your hand
   and satisfy the desire of every living thing. *R/*

3. The LORD is just in all his ways
   and holy in all his works.
   The LORD is near to all who call upon him,
   to all who call upon him in truth. *R/*

17 OT B only

1a. Let all your works give you thanks, O LORD,
and let your faithful ones bless you.
Let them discourse of the glory of your kingdom
and speak of your might. *R/*

18 OT A
1. - 2. - 3.
17 OT B
1a. - 2. - 3.

25th Sunday in Ordinary Time, Year A

Psalm Tone

Psalm 145:2-3, 8-9, 17-18. R/ v. 18a

1. Every day will I bless you,
 and I will praise your name forever and ever.
 Great is the LORD and highly to be praised;
 his greatness is unsearchable. *R/*

2. The LORD is gracious and merciful,
 slow to anger and of great kindness.
 The LORD is good to all
 and compassionate toward all his works. *R/*

3. The LORD is just in all his ways
 and holy in all his works.
 The LORD is near to all who call upon him,
 to all who call upon him in truth. *R/*

Psalm 146

23rd Sunday in Ordinary Time, Year B • 32nd Sunday in Ordinary Time, Year B • 26th Sunday in Ordinary Time, Year C

3rd Sunday of Advent, Year A, *alternate response* • 23rd Sunday in Ordinary Time, Year B, *alternate response* • 32nd Sunday in Ordinary Time, Year B, *alternate response* • 26th Sunday in Ordinary Time, Year C, *alternate response*

4th Sunday in Ordinary Time, Year A

3rd Sunday of Advent, Year A

Psalm Tone

Psalm 146:6-7, 8-9, 9-10. R/ v. 1b; Mt 5:3; cf. Is 35:4

1. The Lord keeps faith forever,
   secures justice for the oppressed,
   gives food to the hungry.
   The Lord sets captives free. *R/*

2. The Lord gives sight to the blind;
   the Lord raises up those who were bowed down.
   The Lord loves the just;
   the Lord protects strangers. *R/*

3. The fatherless and the widow the Lord sustains,
   but the way of the wicked he thwarts.
   The Lord shall reign forever;
   your God, O Zion, through all generations. Alleluia. *R/*

3 Adv A, v. 1, line 1
1. The Lord God keeps faith forever,

23 OT B, v. 1, line 1
1. The God of Jacob keeps faith forever,

26 OT C, v. 1, line 1
1. Blessed he who keeps faith forever.

3 Adv A, v. 3, line 4
your God, O Zion, through all generations. *R/*

Note:
32 OT B and ***26 OT C*** have minor differences of punctuation in v. 2.

Psalm 147a

5th Sunday in Ordinary Time, Year B

5th Sunday in Ordinary Time, Year B, *alternate response*

Psalm Tone

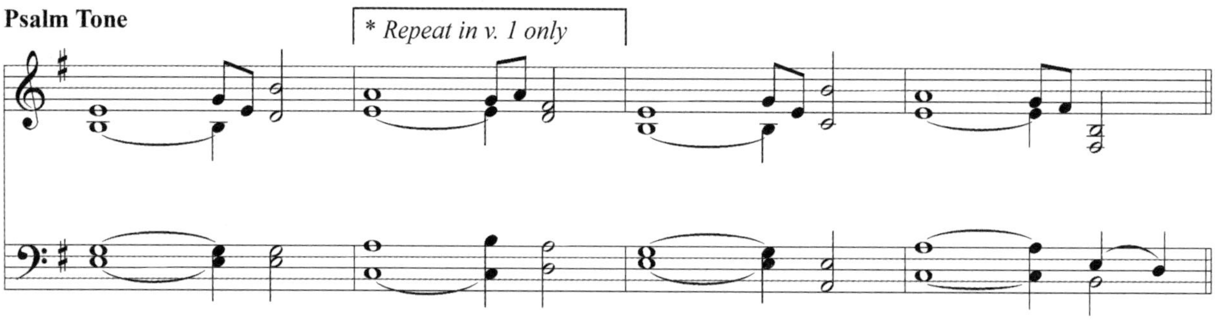

Psalm 147:1-2, 3-4, 5-6 R/ cf. v. 3a

1. Praise the LORD, for he is good;
   sing praise to our God, for he is gracious;
   * it is fitting to praise him.
   The LORD rebuilds Jerusalem;
   the dispersed of Israel he gathers. *R/*

2. He heals the brokenhearted
   and binds up their wounds.
   He tells the number of the stars;
   he calls each by name. *R/*

3. Great is our Lord and mighty in power;
   to his wisdom there is no limit.
   The LORD sustains the lowly;
   the wicked he casts to the ground. *R/*

Psalm 147b

Body and Blood of Christ, Year A

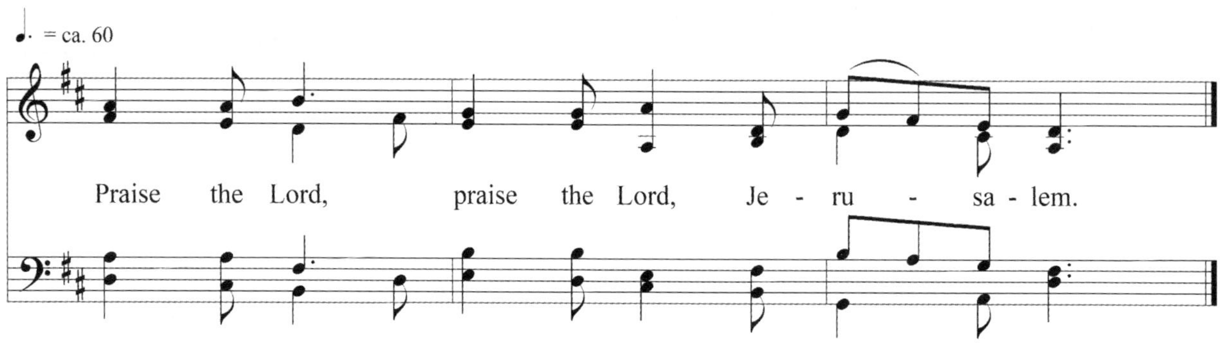

2nd Sunday after Christmas

Body and Blood of Christ, Year A, *alternate response* •
2nd Sunday after Christmas, *alternate response*

Psalm Tone

Psalm 147:12-13, 14-15, 19-20. R/ v. 12; Jn 1:14

1. Glorify the Lord, <u>O</u> Jerusalem;
   praise your <u>God</u>, O Zion.
   For he has strengthened the bars <u>of</u> your gates;
   he has blessed your chil<u>dren</u> within you. *R/*

2. He has granted peace <u>in</u> your borders;
   with the best of <u>wheat</u> he fills you.
   He sends forth his command <u>to</u> the earth;
   swiftly <u>runs</u> his word! *R/*

3. He has proclaimed his <u>word</u> to Jacob,
   his statutes and his ordinanc<u>es</u> to Israel.
   He has not done thus for any <u>o</u>ther nation;
   his ordinances he has not made known to them. <u>Al</u>leluia. *R/*

Exodus 15

Easter Vigil 3

Canticle Tone

Exodus 15:1-2, 3-4, 5-6, 17-18. R/ v. 1b

1. I will sing to the Lord, for he is gloriously triumphant;
 horse and chariot he has cast into the sea.
 My strength and my courage is the Lord,
 and he has been my savior.
 He is my God, I praise him;
 the God of my father, I extol him. *R/*

2. The Lord is a warrior,
 Lord is his name!
 Pharaoh's chariots and army he hurled into the sea;
 ** [*Omit mm. 4-5*]
 the elite of his officers were submerged in the Red Sea. *R/*

3. The flood waters covered them,
 they sank into the depths like a stone.
 Your right hand, O Lord, magnificent in power,
 your right hand, O Lord, has shattered the enemy. *R/*

4. You brought in the people you redeemed
 and planted them on the mountain of your inheritance
 the place where you made your seat, O Lord,
 the sanctuary, Lord, which your hands established.
 * [*Omit m. 5*]
 The Lord shall reign forever and ever. *R/*

Note:
Since 1970, the U.S. Lectionary has contained an important error at the end of the Exodus reading preceding this canticle.

According to the Latin original, the reading should end with "Then Moses and the Israelites sang this song to the Lord:" (last line but two), and the Canticle then follows **immediately**, with **no other** lines of scripture and **no** concluding formula ("The word of the Lord") intervening.

1 Chronicles

Thanksgiving, option 1 • Anniversary of Dedication, option 1

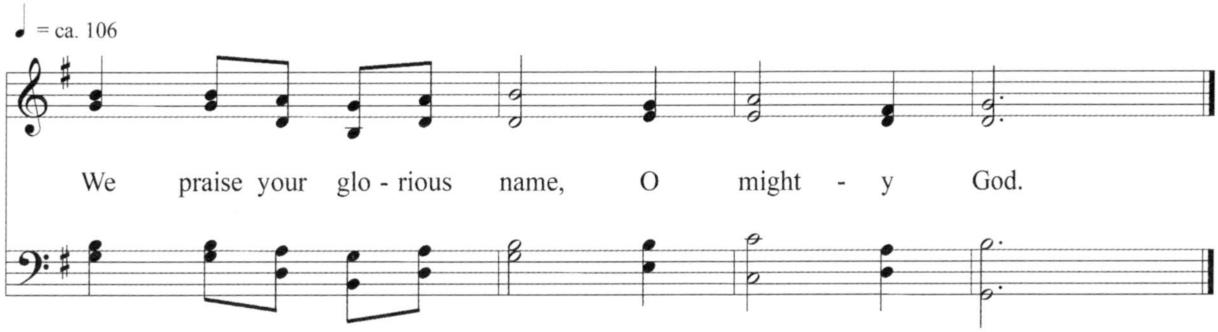

Canticle Tone

1 Chronicles 29:10bcd, 11abc, 11d-12a, 12bcd. R/ v. 13b

1. "Blessed may you be, O LORD,
   God of Israel our father,
   from eternity to eternity." *R/*

2. "Yours, O LORD, are grandeur and power,
   majesty, splendor, and glory.
   For all in heaven and on earth is yours." *R/*

3. "Yours, O LORD, is the sovereignty;
   you are exalted as head over all.
   Riches and honor are from you." *R/*

4. "You have dominion over all,
   In your hand are power and might;
   it is yours to give grandeur and strength to all." *R/*

Isaiah 12

Easter Vigil 5 • Easter Vigil 7, *alternate psalm* • Baptism of the Lord, Year B • Sacred Heart, Year B

3rd Sunday of Advent, Year C

Canticle Tone

Isaiah 12:2-3, 4, 5-6. R/ v. 6

1. God indeed is my savior;
   I am confident and unafraid.
   My strength and my courage is the Lord,
   and he has been my savior.
   With joy you will draw water
   at the fountain of salvation. *R/*

2. Give thanks to the Lord,
   acclaim his name;
   among the nations make known his deeds,
   proclaim how exalted is his name. *R/*
   ** [*Omit mm. 5-6*]

3. Sing praise to the Lord
   for his glorious achievement;
   let this be known throughout all the earth.
   Shout with exultation, O city of Zion,
   for great in your midst
   is the Holy One of Israel! *R/*

Daniel 3

Pentecost Vigil 2 • Trinity, Year A

Canticle Tone

Daniel 3:52, 53, 54, 55, 56. R/ v. 52b

1. Blessed are you, O LORD, the God of our fathers,
   praiseworthy and exalted above all forever;
   and blessed is your holy and glorious name,
   praiseworthy and exalted above all for all ages. *R/*

2. ** [*Omit mm. 1-2*]
   Blessed are you in the temple of your holy glory,
   praiseworthy and glorious above all forever. *R/*

3. ** [*Omit mm. 1-2*]
   Blessed are you on the throne of your kingdom,
   praiseworthy and exalted above all forever. *R/*

4. Blessed are you who look into the depths
   from your throne upon the cherubim,
   * [*Omit m. 3*]
   praiseworthy and exalted above all forever. *R/*

Luke 1

3rd Sunday of Advent, Year B

Canticle Tone

Luke 1:46-48, 49-50, 53-54. R/ cf. Is 61:10b

1. My soul proclaims the greatness of the Lord;
 my spirit rejoices in God my Savior,
 for he has looked upon his lowly servant.
 From this day all generations will call me blessed: *R/*

2. the Almighty has done great things for me,
 and holy is his Name.
 He has mercy on those who fear him
 in every generation. *R/*

3. He has filled the hungry with good things,
 and the rich he has sent away empty.
 He has come to the help of his servant Israel
 for he has remembered his promise of mercy. *R/*

Liturgical Index by Use

NB: references are to Psalm number, not page number

Canticles are Ex (Exodus), 1 Chron (1 Chronicles), Is (Isaiah), Dan (Daniel), Lk (Luke)

See note at end re: Psalm 147a and Psalm 147b

Liturgical Day	*Year A*	*Year B*	*Year C*
	PROPER OF TIME		
1st Sunday of Advent	122	80	25
2nd Sunday of Advent	72	85	126
3rd Sunday of Advent	146	Lk 1	Is 12
4th Sunday of Advent	24	89	80
Christmas Vigil	89	89	89
Christmas Midnight	96	96	96
Christmas Dawn	97	97	97
Christmas Day	98	98	98
Holy Family	128	105	84
Mary, Mother of God	67	67	67
2nd Sunday after Christmas	147b+	147b+	147b+
Epiphany Vigil	72	72	72
Epiphany Day	72	72	72
Baptism of the Lord	29	Is 12	104
Ash Wednesday	51	51	51
1st Sunday of Lent	51	25	91
2nd Sunday of Lent	33	116	27
3rd Sunday of Lent	95	19	103
4th Sunday of Lent	23	137	34
5th Sunday of Lent	130	51	126
Palm Sunday	22	22	22
Holy Thursday Evening	116	116	116
Good Friday	31	31	31
Easter Vigil			
Psalm 1	104	104	104
Psalm 1 *alternate*	33	33	33
Psalm 2	16	16	16
Psalm 3	Ex 15	Ex 15	Ex 15
Psalm 4	30	30	30
Psalm 5	Is 12	Is 12	Is 12
Psalm 6	19	19	19
Psalm 7	42-3	42-3	42-3
Psalm 7 *alternate 1*	Is 12	Is 12	Is 12
Psalm 7 *alternate 2*	51	51	51
Alleluia Psalm	118	118	118
Easter Day	118	118	118
2nd Sunday of Easter	118	118	118

Liturgical Day	*Year A*	*Year B*	*Year C*
3rd Sunday of Easter	16	4	30
4th Sunday of Easter	23	118	100
5th Sunday of Easter	33	22	145
6th Sunday of Easter	66	98	67
Ascension Vigil and Day	47	47	47
7th Sunday of Easter	27	103	97
Pentecost Extended Vigil			
Psalm 1	33	33	33
Psalm 2	Dan 3	Dan 3	Dan 3
Psalm 2 *alternate*	19	19	19
Psalm 3	107	107	107
Psalm 4 (& Simple Vigil)	104	104	104
Pentecost Day	104	104	104
Trinity Sunday	Dan 3	33	8
Body and Blood of Christ	147b+	116	110
Sacred Heart	103	Is 12	23
2nd Sunday in Ordinary Time	40	40	96
3rd Sunday in Ordinary Time	27	25	19
4th Sunday in Ordinary Time	146	95	71
5th Sunday in Ordinary Time	112	147a+	138
6th Sunday in Ordinary Time	119	32	1
7th Sunday in Ordinary Time	103	41	103
8th Sunday in Ordinary Time	62	103	92
9th Sunday in Ordinary Time	31	81	117
10th Sunday in Ordinary Time	50	130	30
11th Sunday in Ordinary Time	100	92	32
12th Sunday in Ordinary Time	69	107	63
13th Sunday in Ordinary Time	89	30	16
14th Sunday in Ordinary Time	145	123	66
15th Sunday in Ordinary Time	65	85	69
15th Sunday in Ordinary Time *alternate*			19
16th Sunday in Ordinary Time	86	23	15
17th Sunday in Ordinary Time	119	145	138
18th Sunday in Ordinary Time	145	78	90
18th Sunday in Ordinary Time *alternate*			[95]*
19th Sunday in Ordinary Time	85	34	33
20th Sunday in Ordinary Time	67	34	40
21st Sunday in Ordinary Time	138	34	117
22nd Sunday in Ordinary Time	63	15	68
23rd Sunday in Ordinary Time	95	146	90
24th Sunday in Ordinary Time	103	116	51
25th Sunday in Ordinary Time	145	54	113
26th Sunday in Ordinary Time	25	19	146
27th Sunday in Ordinary Time	80	128	95
28th Sunday in Ordinary Time	23	90	98
29th Sunday in Ordinary Time	96	33	121

Liturgical Day	*Year A*	*Year B*	*Year C*
30th Sunday in Ordinary Time	18	126	34
31st Sunday in Ordinary Time	131	18	145
32nd Sunday in Ordinary Time	63	146	17
33rd Sunday in Ordinary Time	128	16	98
Christ the King	23	93	122

COMMON PSALMS

(may replace the psalm proper to a particular day)

Common Psalm Advent 1	25
Common Psalm Advent 2	85
Common Psalm Christmas	98
Common Psalm Epiphany	72
Common Psalm Lent 1	51
Common Psalm Lent 2	91
Common Psalm Lent 3	130
Common Psalm Holy Week	22
Common Psalm Easter Vigil 1	136
Common Psalm Easter Vigil 2	136
Common Psalm Easter Season 1	118
Common Psalm Easter Season 2	66
Common Psalm Ascension	47
Common Psalm Pentecost	104
Common Psalm Ordinary Time 1	19
Common Psalm Ordinary Time 2	27
Common Psalm Ordinary Time 3	34
Common Psalm Ordinary Time 4	63
Common Psalm Ordinary Time 5	95
Common Psalm Ordinary Time 6	100
Common Psalm Ordinary Time 7	103
Common Psalm Ordinary Time 8	145
Common Psalm Ordinary Time 9 (last weeks)	122

PROPER OF SAINTS and OTHER DAYS WHICH MAY REPLACE A SUNDAY

Liturgical Day	*Years A, B, and C*		
February 2: Presentation of the Lord	24		
March 25: Annunciation of the B.V.M.	40		
June 23: St John the Baptist (Vigil)	71		
June 24: St John the Baptist (Day)	139		
June 28: Ss Peter and Paul (Vigil)	19		
June 29: Ss Peter and Paul (Day)	34		
August 6: Transfiguration of the Lord	97		
August 14: Assumption of the B.V.M. (Vigil)	132		
August 15: Assumption of the B.V.M. (Day)	45		
September 14: Exaltation of the Holy Cross	78		
November 1: All Saints	24		
November 2: All Souls (three Masses)	23	25	27

Liturgical Day		*Years A, B, and C*			
November 9: Dedication of the Lateran Basilica		46			
December 8: Immaculate Conception of the B.V.M.		98			
Thanksgiving Day (Lectionary psalms)		1 Chron	113	138	145
Thanksgiving Day (C.E. alternate psalm)**		67			
Anniversary of Dedication of a Church,	option 1	1 Chron			
	option 2	46			
	option 3	84			
	option 4	95			
	option 5	122			

* (**18 OT C** was Psalm 95 in original 1970 Lectionary)

** C.E. = *Celebrating the Eucharist*

+ Psalm 147a is Ps 146 in the Vulgate; Psalm 147b is Ps 147 in the Vulgate. We have treated them as separate psalms.

Numerical Index of Psalm Tones

Convert pitches to numbers 1-7, ignoring any accidentals. For example, in C major, C = 1, D = 2, E = 3, and so on. For minor keys, use the relative major. For example, in A minor, A = 6, B = 7, C = 1, and so on.

Tone	Psalm
1121176	105
1216545	23
1217654	27
1232234	145
1234234	50
1234256	80
1234561	1
1345353	92
1261721	139
1423125	138
1612611	68
1671212	51
1712212	71
1712234	136
1716212	72
1761712	126
1767656	91

Tone	Psalm
2321223	66
2324313	81
2342316	17
2343456	33 84 128
2345246	98
2432354	30
2712312	46

Tone	Psalm
3213216	146
3221721	54 variant of Ps 41 following
3221446	41 130 137 (variant)
3234543	4
3423454	90 95 113
3432121	34 96
3432161	62
3432232	67
3432543	85
3436676	69
3452123	104
3454346	78
3456234	93 97 119 *Dan 3*
3456523	116
3463616	22 31
3521376	65
3532131	118 132
3565233	110
3654254	122

Tone	Psalm
4321612	18 89
4345764	45
4543212	63
4635765	15
4671176	123

Tone	Psalm
5356424	147b
5364253	19
5366171	100
5431216	40
5432313	*Lk 1*
5517455	117
5615131	22
5635341	112
5656432	*Ex 15 Is 12*
5675542	24

Tone	Psalm
6125645	8
6162354	121
6163212	147a
6167566	131
6542361	32
6566561	86
6712123	25
6713212	103
6716176	107
6716217	42-3
6723212	16
6723345	29

Index of Psalm Tones by Category and Key

Convert pitches to numbers 1-7, ignoring any accidentals. For example, in C major, C = 1, D = 2, E = 3, and so on. For minor keys, use the relative major. For example, in A minor, A = 6, B = 7, C = 1, and so on.

2-line chants

E flat major	4345764	Ps 45

3-line chants

C major	3456234	Ps 97 (see also E flat major, 4-line chants C major)
C major	5366171	Ps 100
E flat major	3456234	Ps 93 (see also C major, 4-line chants C major)
E flat major	3565233	Ps 110
F major	3234543	Ps 4
G major	3215616	1 Chron

4-line chants

A major	1216545	Ps 23
A minor	4543212	Ps 63
A minor	6175645	Ps 8
B flat major	1121176	Ps 105
B flat major	1217654	Ps 27
B flat major	1612611	Ps 68
B flat major	3456523	Ps 116
C major	2343456	Ps 33 Ps 84 Ps 128
C major	3456234	Ps 97 Ps 119 (see also D major) (see also 3-line chants C major and E flat major)
C major	5176621	Ps 47
C major	*5615131	Ps 22 Ps 31 (for minor version, see asterisked line below)
C major	5675542	Ps 24
C major	6542361	Ps 32
C minor	1261721	Ps 139 (see also E flat major) (see also 5-line chants)
C minor	*3463616	Ps 22 Ps 31 (for major version, see asterisked line above)
D major	1234236	Ps 80
D major	1712234	Ps 136
D major	2345246	Ps 98
D major	3456234	Dan 3 (see also C major) (see also 3-line chants C major and E flat major)
D major	5174541	Ps 117
D major	5356424	Ps 147b
D major	5431216	Ps 40 (see also E flat major)
D minor	1651212	Ps 51
D minor	3221721	Ps 54 (for variant, see following entry)
D minor	3221446	Ps 41 Ps 130 (for variant, see preceding entry) (see also E minor)
D minor	3432543	Ps 85
D minor	3452123	Ps 104
D minor	6723345	Ps 29
E flat major	1232234	Ps 145
E flat major	1261721	Ps 139 (see also C minor) (see also 5-line chants)
E flat major	2342316	Ps 17

5-line chants

6-line chants

Index of First Lines of Psalm Extracts

Entries are in strictly alphabetical order, ignoring any punctuation or gaps between words

References are to Psalm numbers, not page numbers
Where a psalm has several extracts, the first line of each one is listed if it begins differently

Canticles are Ex 15 (Exodus), 1 Chron (1 Chronicles), Is 12 (Isaiah), Dan 3 (Daniel), Lk 1 (Luke)

Index of First Lines of Responses

Entries are in strictly alphabetical order, ignoring any punctuation or gaps between words

References are to Psalm numbers, not page numbers

Canticles are Ex 15 (Exodus), 1 Chron (1 Chronicles), Is 12 (Isaiah), Dan 3 (Daniel), Lk 1 (Luke)